budgetbooks

LOVE SONGS

ISBN: 978-0-634-04071-9

HAL•LEONARD®
CORPORATION

7777 W. BLUEMOUND RD. P.O. BOX 13819 MILWAUKEE, WI 53213

Visit Hal Leonard Online at
www.halleonard.com

CONTENTS

ALL MY LOVING

Words and Music by JOHN LENNON
and PAUL McCARTNEY

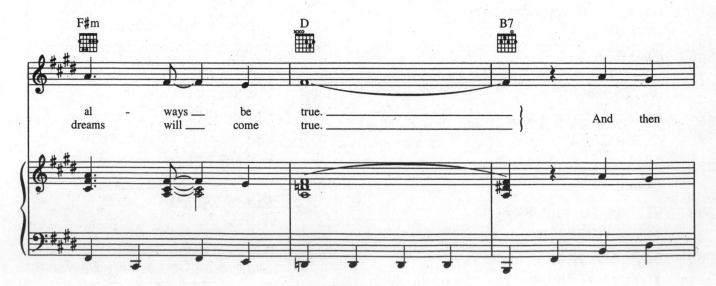

ALL OR NOTHING

Words and Music by WAYNE HECTOR
and STEVE MAC

know when he's been on your mind, __ the dis-tant look is in your eyes, __ I
There are times it seems to me __ I'm shar-ing you with mem-o-ries. __ I

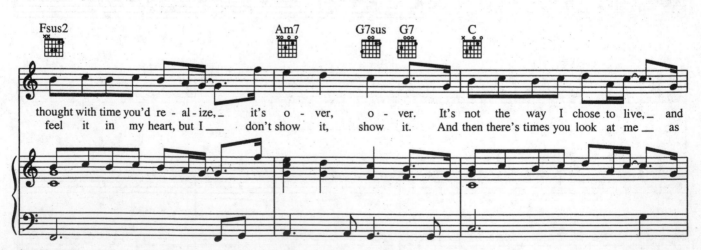

thought with time you'd re-al-ize, __ it's o-ver, o-ver. It's not the way I chose to live, __ and
feel it in my heart, but I __ don't show it, show it. And then there's times you look at me __ as

9

fall when you reach the bot - tom; it's now or nev - er. Is it

all, or are we ___ just ___ friends? ___ Is this how ___ it

ends, with a sim - ple tel - e - phone call? You leave me here with noth - ing at

all.   leave me here with noth - ing. ___ 'Cause

you and I _____ could lose it all if you've got no more room, no

room in sight _____ for me in your life. _____ 'Cause I want it

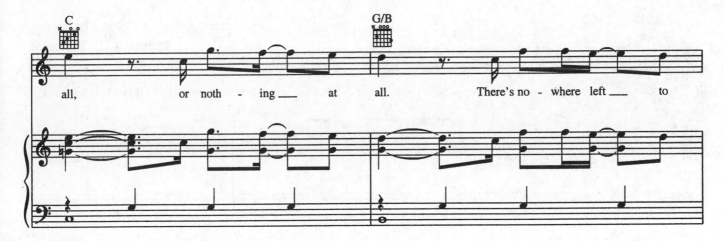

all, or noth-ing ___ at all. There's no-where left ___ to

fall; it's now or nev-er. Is it

all,   or noth - ing ___ at all.   There's no - where left ___ to

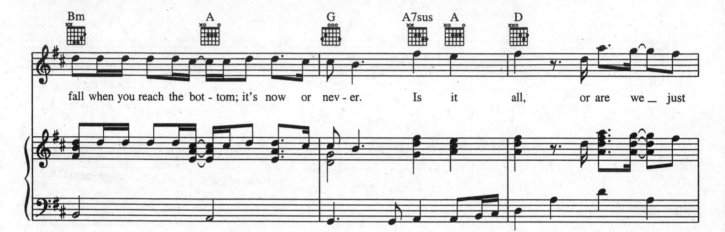

fall when you reach the bot - tom; it's now or nev - er. Is it   all,   or are we ___ just

friends? ___ Is this how. it ends, with a sim - ple tel - e-phone call? You leave me here with noth - ing at

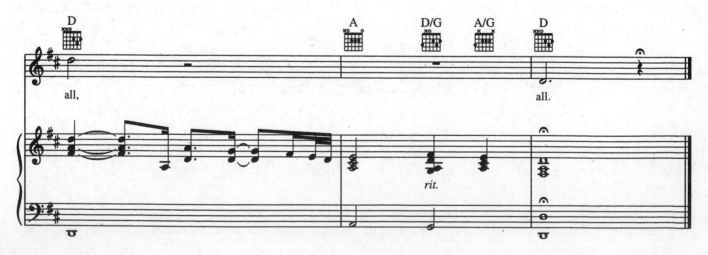

all,   all.

ALWAYS

Words and Music by GARY CHAPMAN
and MICHAEL W. SMITH

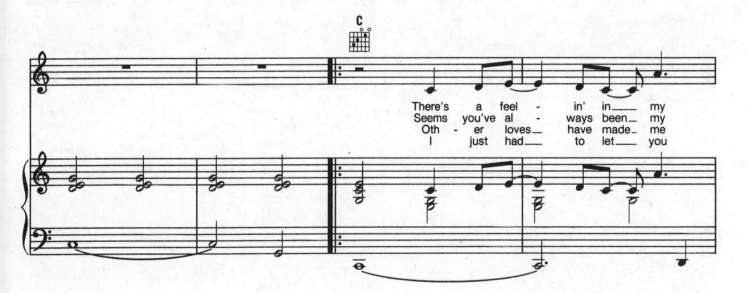

There's a feel - in' in___ my
Seems you've al - ways been___ my
Oth - er loves___ have made me
I just had___ to let___ you

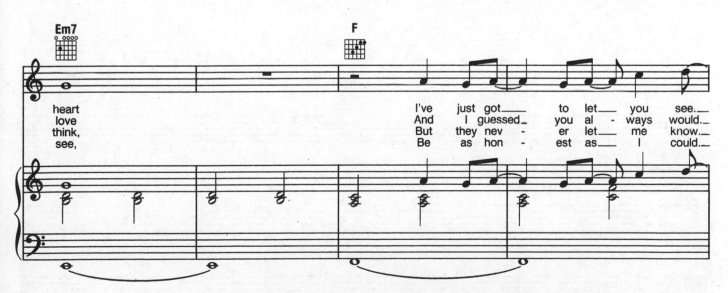

heart
love
think,
see,

I've just got___ to let___ you see.___
And I guessed___ you al - ways would.___
But they nev - er let___ me know.___
Be as hon - est as___ I could.___

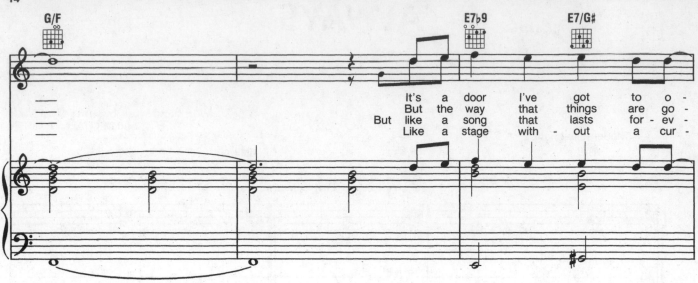

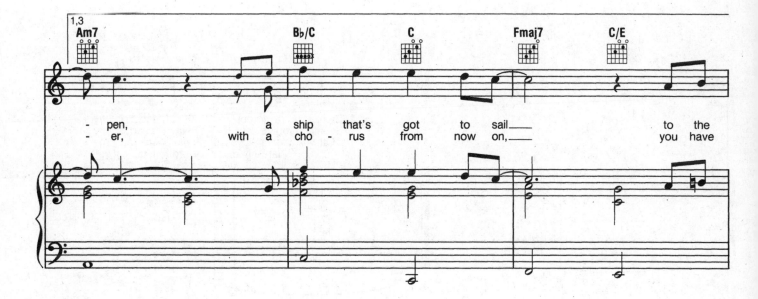

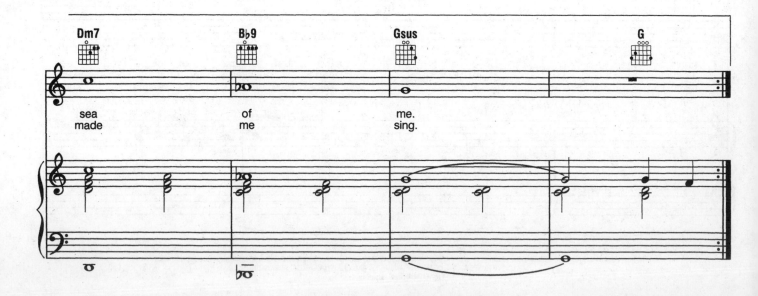

AND I LOVE HER

Words and Music by JOHN LENNON
and PAUL McCARTNEY

I give her all _____ my love, _____
She gives me ev - 'ry - thing _____
Bright are the stars _____ that shine, _____

that's all I do. _____
and ten - der - ly. _____
dark is the sky. _____

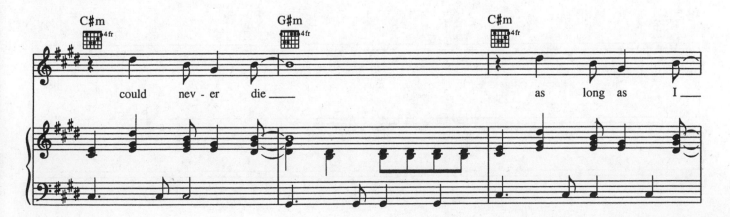

D.S. al Coda

have you near _ me. _____

CODA

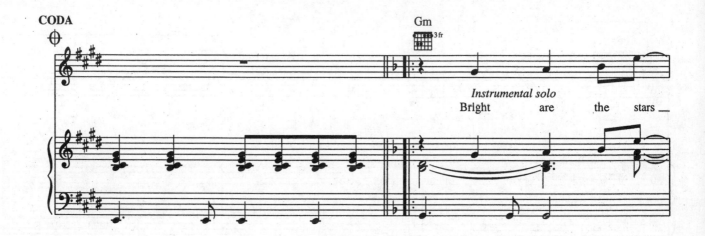

Instrumental solo

Bright are the stars _

_ that shine, _   dark is the sky. _____

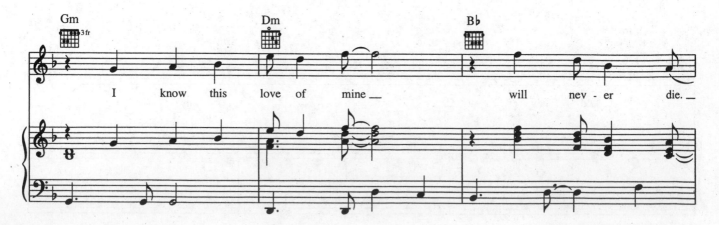

I know this love of mine _   will nev - er die. _

End instrumental solo

And I love

her.

ANYTIME YOU NEED A FRIEND

Words and Music by MARIAH CAREY
and WALTER AFANASIEFF

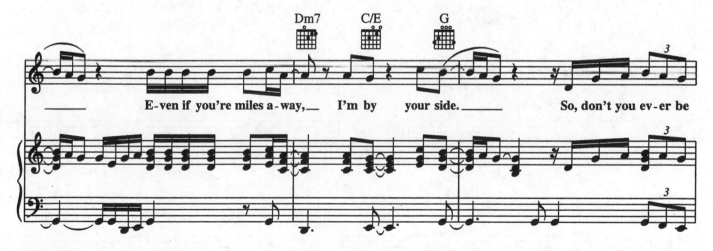

BABY LOVE

Words and Music by BRIAN HOLLAND,
EDWARD HOLLAND and LAMONT DOZIER

Ba - by love, my ba - by love, I need you oh how I need you.
Ba - by love, my ba - by love, why must we sep - a - rate my love?
me my love, my ba - by love, I need ya, oh how I need ya.

But all you do is treat me bad, break my heart and leave me sad.
All of my whole life through, I nev - er love no one but you.
Why you do me like you do, af - ter I've been true to you.

Wan - na know what did I do wrong to make you stay a - way so long. 'Cause
Why you do me like you do, I guess it's me ooh. Need to
So deep in love with you. Ba - by, ba - by ooh. 'Til it

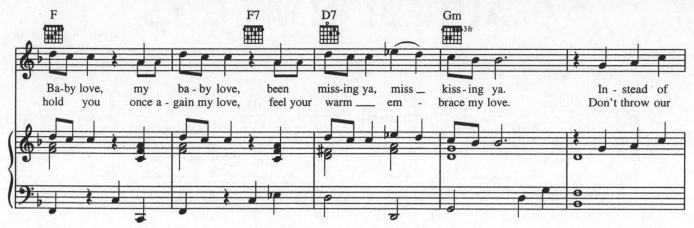

Ba-by love, my ba-by love, been miss-ing ya, miss __ kiss-ing ya. In - stead of
hold you once a - gain my love, feel your warm __ em - brace my love. Don't throw our

break-ing up, ___ let's start some kiss-ing and mak-ing up. ___ Don't throw our
love a - way, ___ please don't do me this way. ___ Not hap-py like I

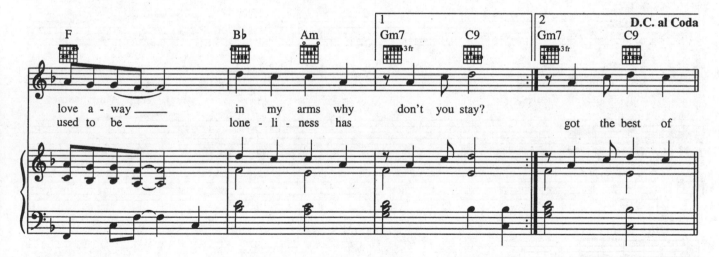

D.C. al Coda

love a - way ___ in my arms why don't you stay?
used to be ___ lone - li - ness has got the best of

Repeat and Fade

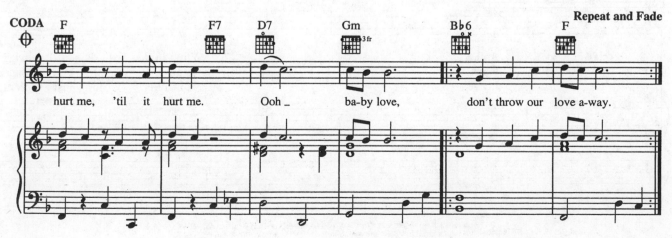

CODA

hurt me, 'til it hurt me. Ooh __ ba-by love, don't throw our love a-way.

BEAUTIFUL IN MY EYES

Words and Music by
JOSHUA KADISON

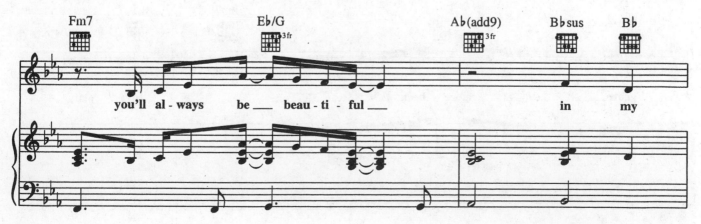

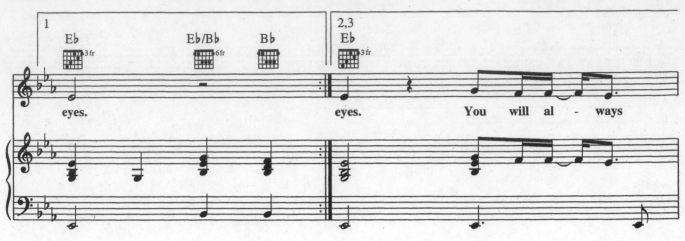

D.S. al Coda
(Take 2nd ending)

eyes.

When there are

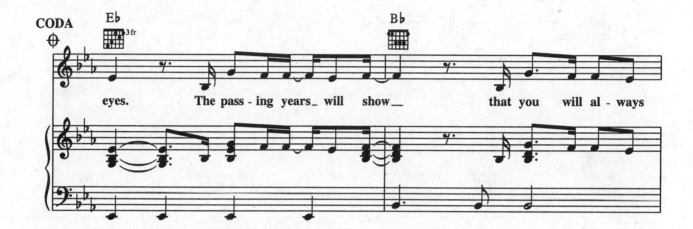

CODA

eyes.   The pass - ing years_ will   show__   that you   will al - ways

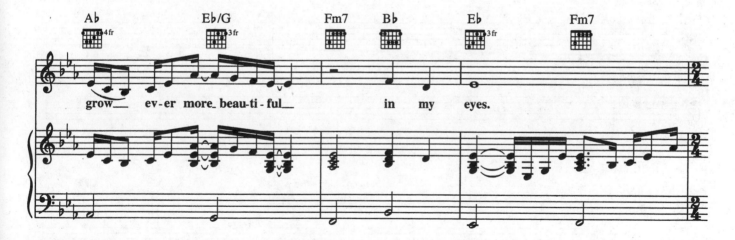

grow__ ev-er more_ beau-ti-ful__   in   my   eyes.

BOTH TO EACH OTHER
(Friends and Lovers)

Words and Music by PAUL GORDON
and JAY GRUSKA

Medium Ballad

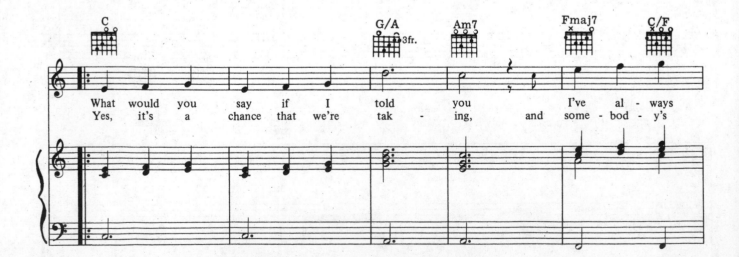

What would you say if I told you I've al- ways
Yes, it's a chance that we're tak- ing, and some-bod- y's

want - ed to hold _____ you. I don't know what we're a - fraid
heart may be break ing. But we can't stop what's in - side

of; nothing would change if we made love. 'Cause I'll
us, our love for each oth - er will guide us.

be your friend, and I'll be your

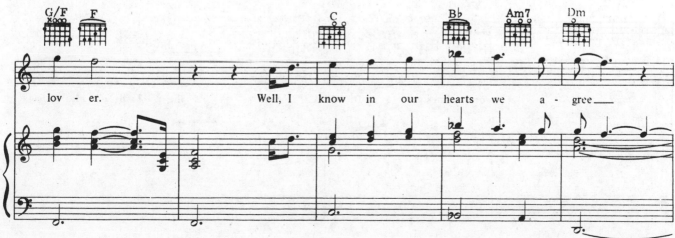

lov - er. Well, I know in our hearts we a - gree _____

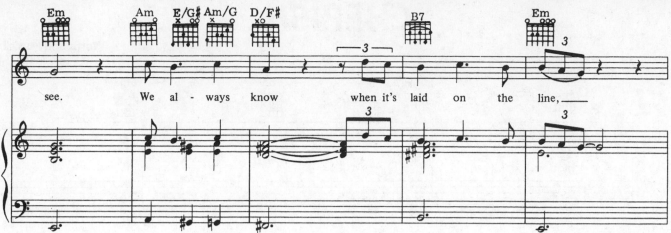

see. We al - ways know when it's laid on the line, ___

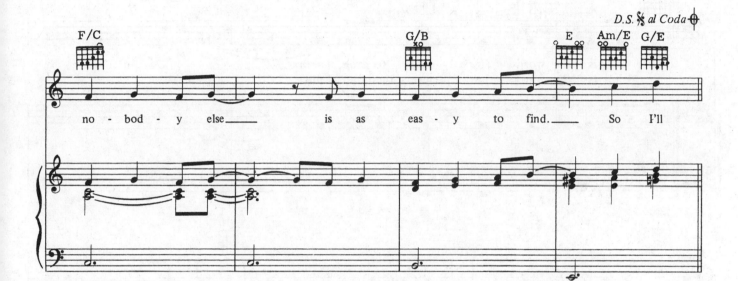

no - bod - y else ___ is as eas - y to find. ___ So I'll

D.S. 𝄋 *al Coda* ⊕

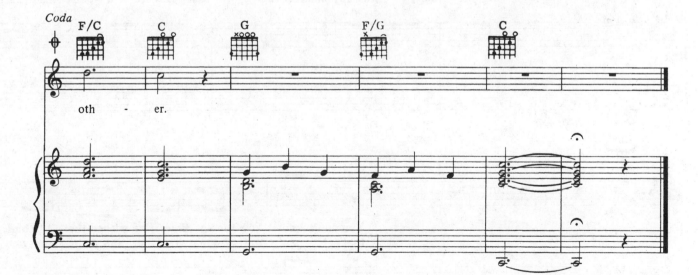

Coda

oth - er.

CHERISH

Words and Music by
TERRY KIRKMAN

40

THE COLOUR OF MY LOVE

Words and Music by DAVID FOSTER
and ARTHUR JANOV

I'll paint my mood in shades of blue,__ paint my soul to be with you.__
I'll draw your arms a-round my waist__ then all doubt I shall e-rase.__

I'll sketch your lips__ in shad-ed tones, draw your mouth to my
I'll paint the rain__ that soft-ly lands on your wind-blown__

42

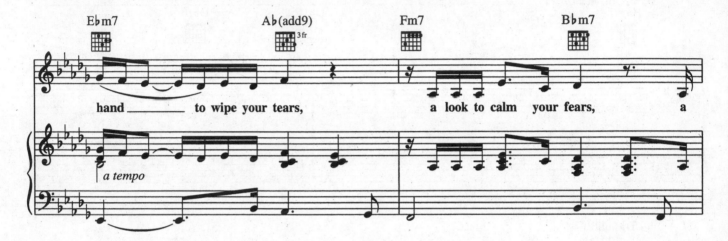

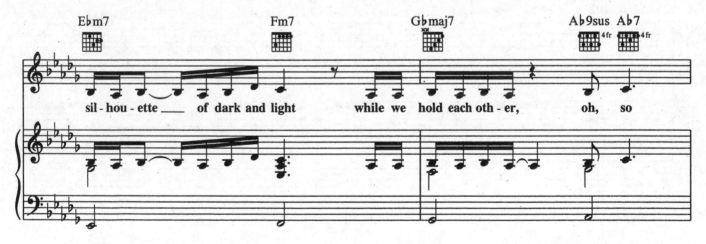

Gbmaj7   Fm7   Bbm7

sun   to warm your heart,   swear-ing that we'll ___ nev - er   part. _____

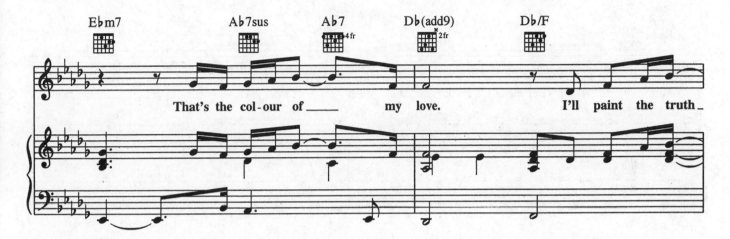

Ebm7   Ab7sus   Ab7   Db(add9)   Db/F

That's the col-our of _____   my   love.   I'll paint the truth _

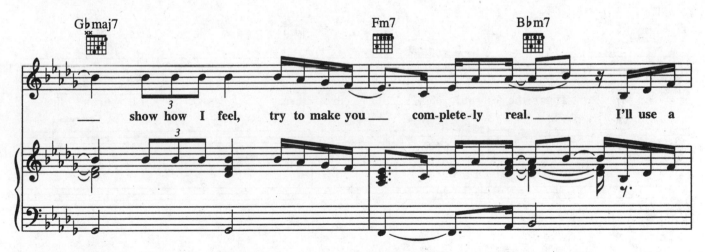

Gbmaj7   Fm7   Bbm7

___ show how I feel,   try to make you ___ com-plete-ly   real. _____   I'll use a

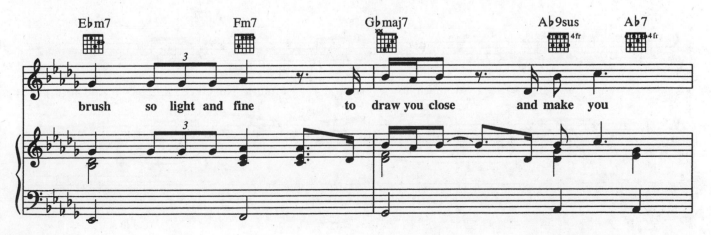

Ebm7   Fm7   Gbmaj7   Ab9sus   Ab7

brush   so light and fine   to draw you close   and make you

44

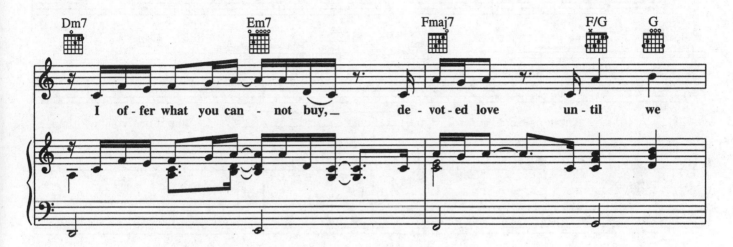

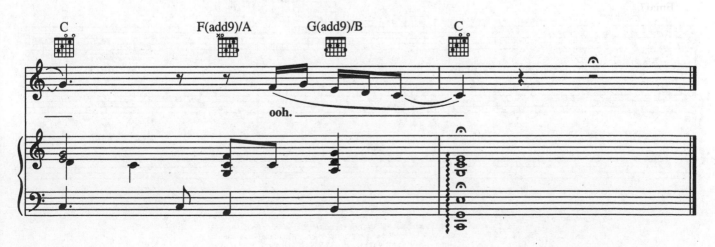

THE CLOSER I GET TO YOU

Words and Music by JAMES MTUME
and REGGIE LUCAS

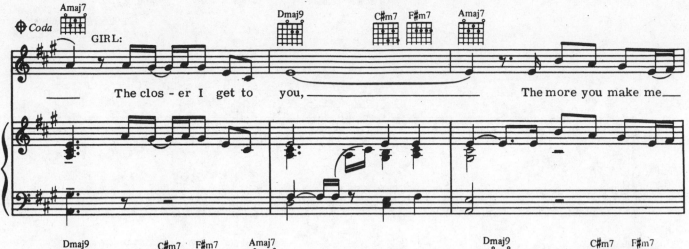

The clos-er I get to you, _____ The more you make me _____

see, _____ By giv-ing you all I've got, _____

_____ Your love ___ has cap-tured ___ me. _____

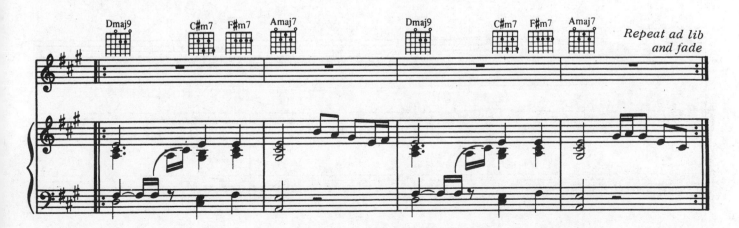

Repeat ad lib and fade

CRAZY

Words and Music by
WILLIE NELSON

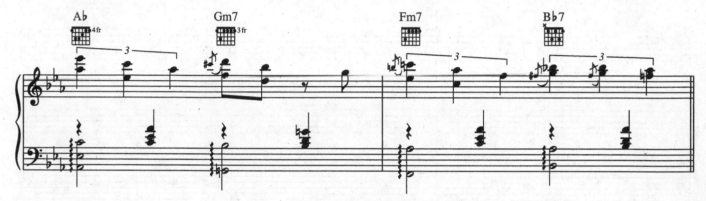

Cra - zy, _____ cra - zy for feel - in' so

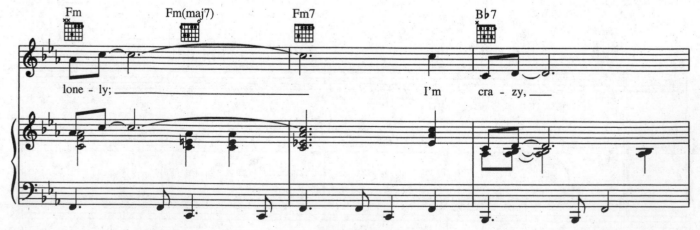

lone - ly; _____ I'm cra - zy, ____

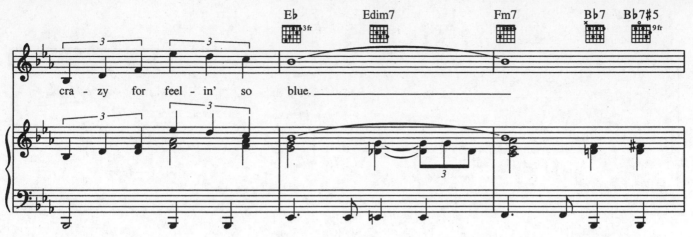

cra - zy for feel - in' so blue. _____

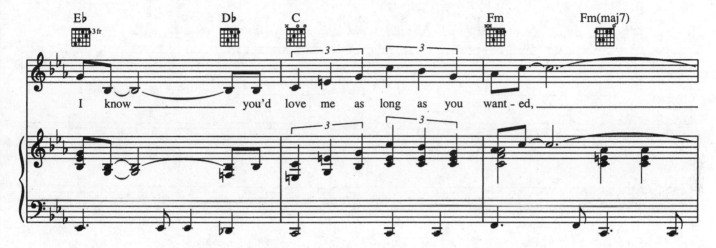

I know _____ you'd love me as long as you want - ed, _____

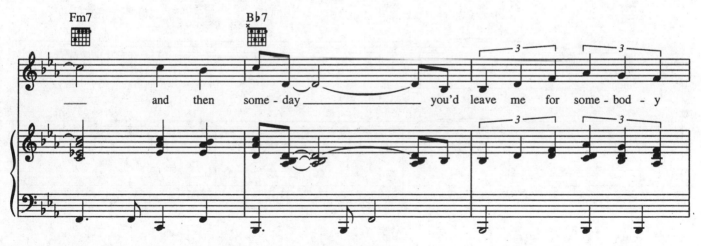

_____ and then some - day _____ you'd leave me for some - bod - y

new. _____ Wor - ry, _____ why do I let my - self

DEDICATED TO THE ONE I LOVE

Words and Music by LOWMAN PAULING
and RALPH BASS

DEJA VU

Lyrics by ADRIENNE ANDERSON
Music by ISAAC HAYES

Moderately slow

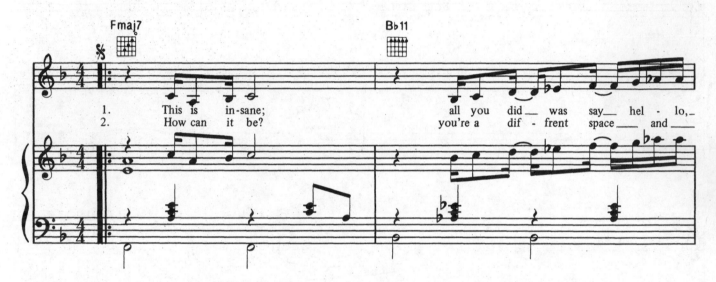

1. This is in-sane;   all you did___ was say___ hel - lo,___
2. How can it be?   you're a dif - frent space___ and ___

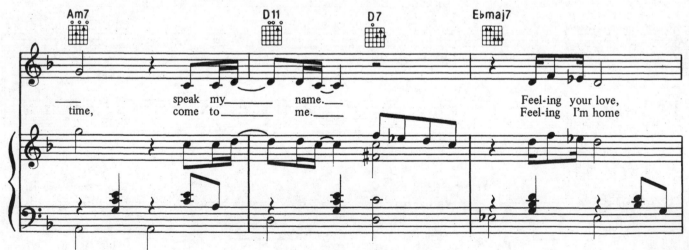

___ time,   speak my_____ name.   Feel-ing your love,
come to_____ me.   Feel-ing I'm home

Additional Verses:

Verse 3   This is divine; I've been waiting all my life, filling time.
Looking for you, nights were more than you could know, long ago.

Verse 4   Come to me now; we don't have to dream of love, we know how.
Somewhere before it's as if I loved you so long ago. *(To Chorus:)*

FIELDS OF GOLD

Written and Composed by
STING

You'll re - mem - ber me when the west wind moves up a -
stay with me, will you be my love a -

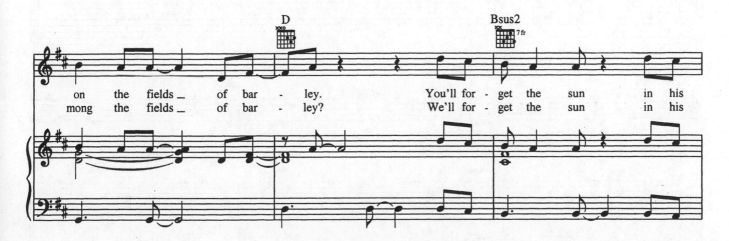

on the fields of bar - ley. You'll for - get the sun in his
mong the fields of bar - ley? We'll for - get the sun in his

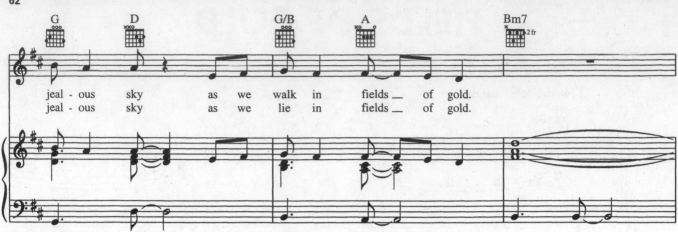

jeal - ous sky   as   we   walk   in   fields ___ of   gold.
jeal - ous sky   as   we   lie   in   fields ___ of   gold.

So she
See the

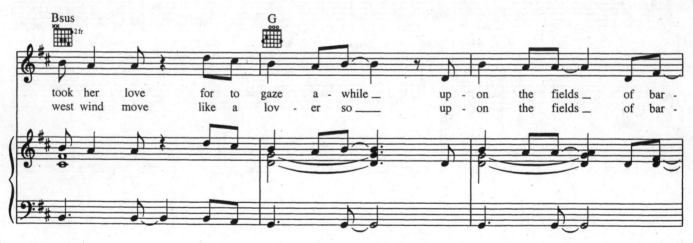

took her love   for to gaze a - while ___   up - on   the fields ___   of bar -
west wind move   like a lov - er so ___   up - on   the fields ___   of bar -

- ley.   In his arms she fell   as her hair came down   a - mong ___
- ley.   Feel her bod - y rise   when you kiss her mouth   a - mong ___

the fields __ of gold.
the fields __ of gold.   Will you

I nev-er made prom-is-es light-ly,   and there have been

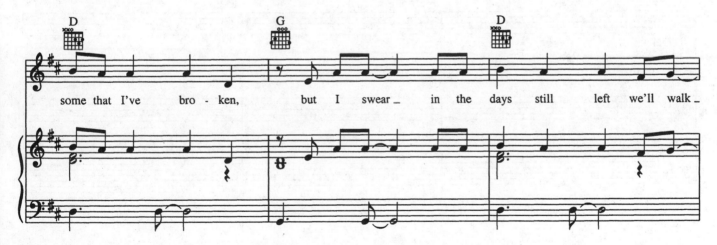

some that I've bro-ken,   but I swear __ in the days still   left we'll walk __

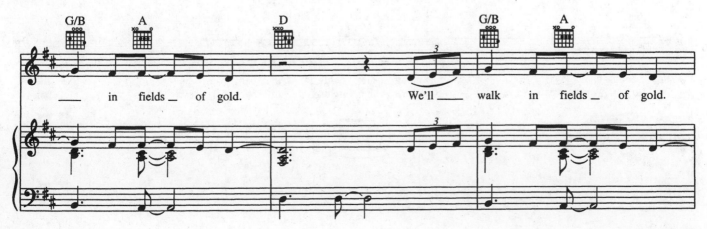

__ in fields __ of gold.   We'll __ walk in fields __ of gold.

64

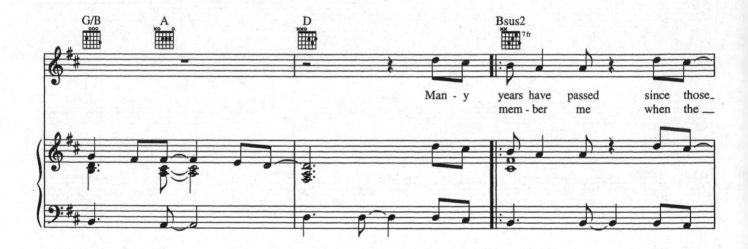

Man - y years have passed since those_
mem - ber me when the _

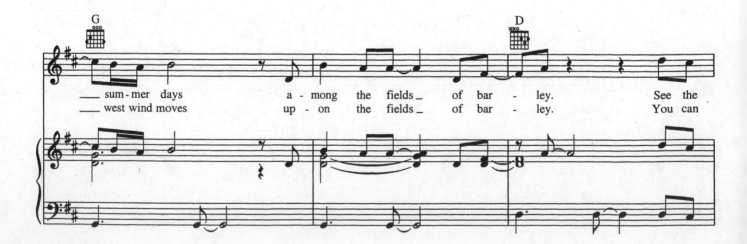

_ sum - mer days a - mong the fields_ of bar - ley. See the
_ west wind moves up - on the fields_ of bar - ley. You can

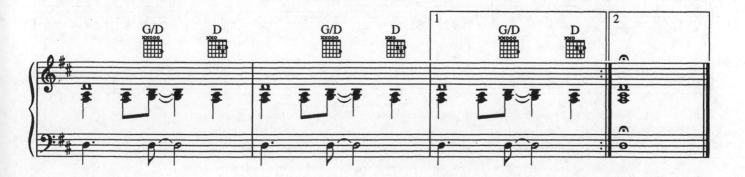

DESTINY

Words and Music by JIM BRICKMAN,
SEAN HOSEIN and DANE DEVILLER

Original key: D-flat major. This edition has been transposed down one half-step to be more playable.
* Male vocal written at pitch.

all my heart ___ and soul, ___ *(Female:)* I give my love to have ___ and hold. __

(Both:) And as far as I ___ can see, ___ you were

al- ways meant __ to be ___ my des - ti - ny.

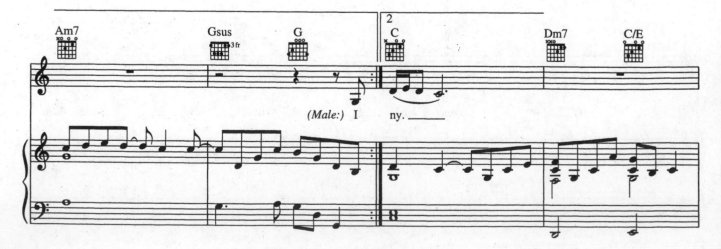

(Male:) I ny. ___

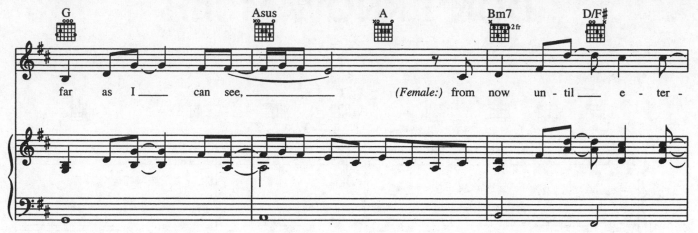

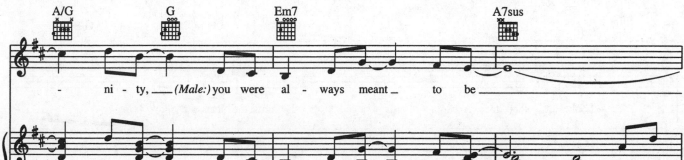

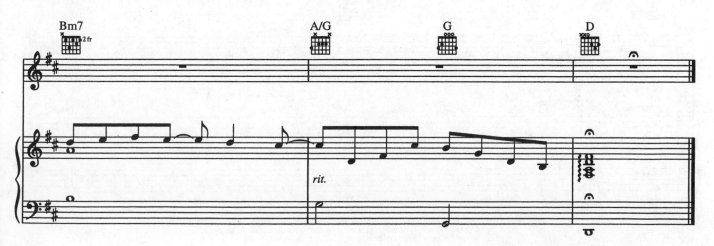

DON'T KNOW MUCH

Words and Music by BARRY MANN,
CYNTHIA WEIL and TOM SNOW

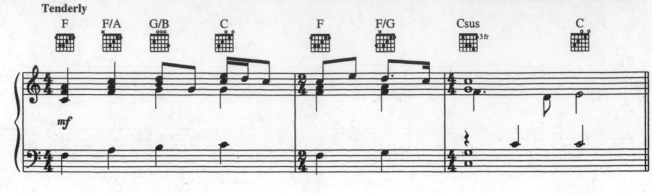

Look at this face, I know the years are show-ing.

Look at this life, ____ I still don't know where ___ it's go-ing.

I don't know ___ much, but I know I love you, _____ and

that may be _____ all I, I need to know.

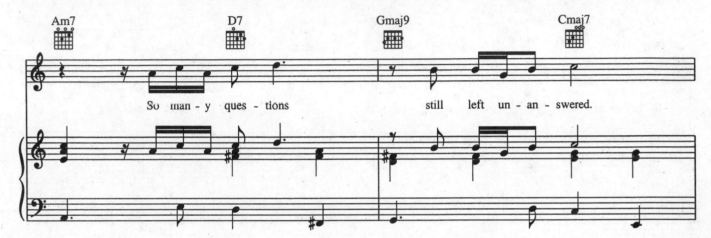

So man-y ques-tions still left un-an-swered.

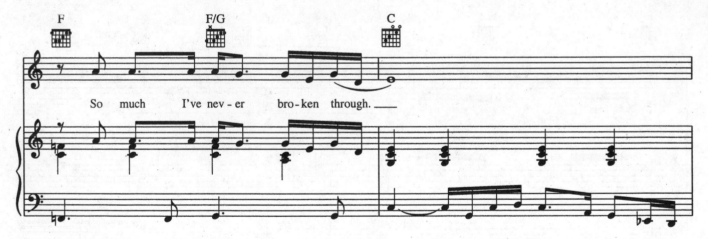

So much I've nev-er bro-ken through. ___

But when I feel you near me some-times I see so clear-ly.

EASY

Words and Music by
LIONEL RICHIE

Know it sounds fun-ny, but I just can't stand the pain.

Girl, I'm leav - ing you ___ to-mor - row. ___

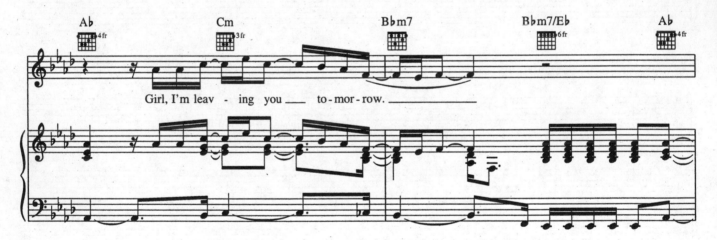

Seems to me, ___ girl, you know I've done all ___ I can.

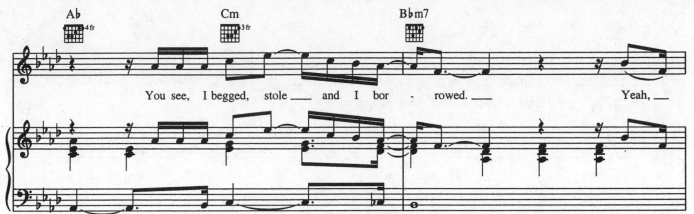

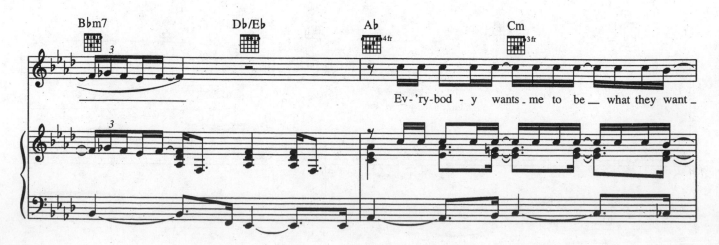

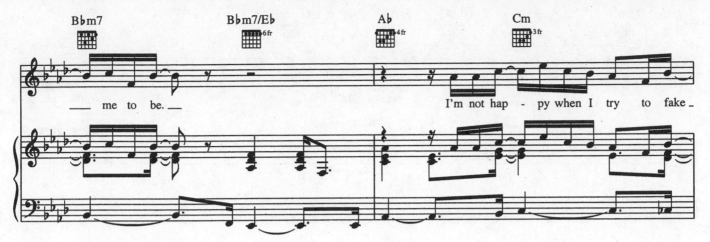

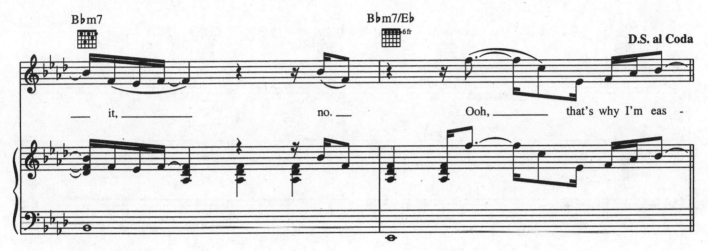

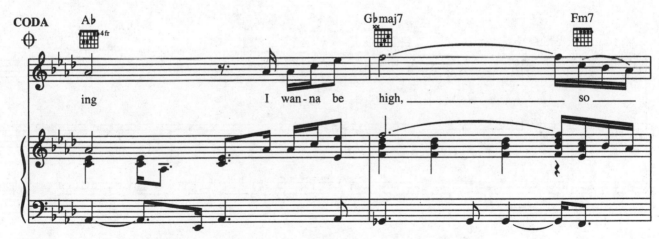

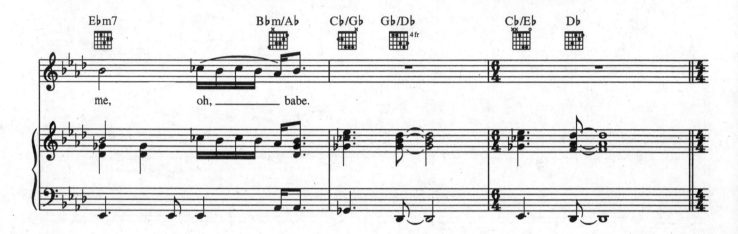

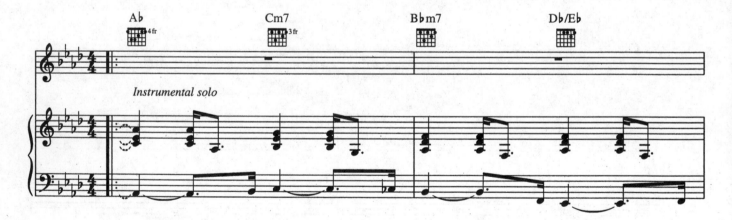

EMOTIONS

Lyrics by MARIAH CAREY
Music by MARIAH CAREY, DAVID COLE and ROBERT CLIVILLES

When you're look-ing in - to _____ my ___ eyes _____ you

make me feel ___ so _____ high! _____

(Vocal 1st time only)

(1st time only)

ENDLESS LOVE

Words and Music by
LIONEL RICHIE

92

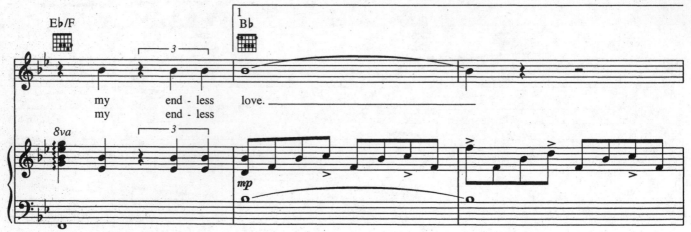

Oh, _____ and _ love, _____

I'll be that fool for ____ you, ____ I'm ____

____ sure; ____ you ____ know I don't mind. ____

And yes, ____ you'll be the

on - ly ____ one. ____ No one can de - ny ____

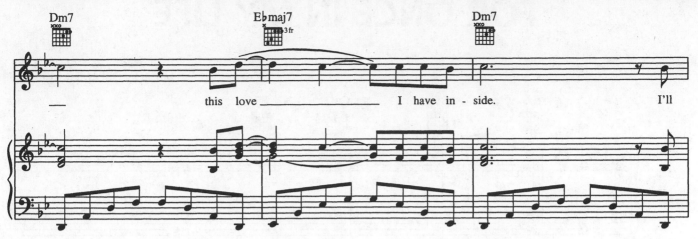

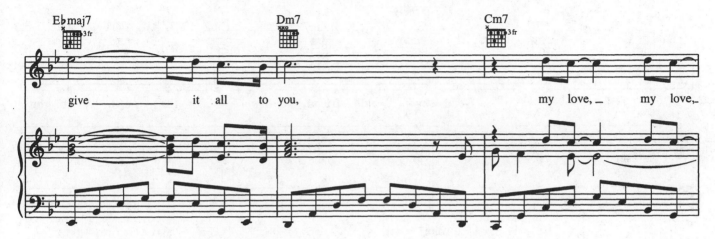

this love _____ I have in-side.   I'll

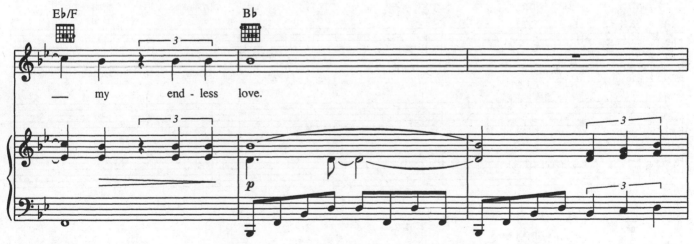

give _____ it all to you,   my love,__ my love,__

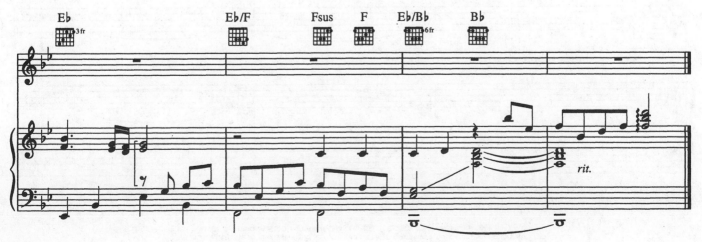

__ my end-less love.

FOR ONCE IN MY LIFE

Words by RONALD MILLER
Music by ORLANDO MURDEN

98

A GROOVY KIND OF LOVE

Words and Music by TONI WINE
and CAROLE BAYER SAGER

breath - ing____ in____ my____ ear.
quiv - er - ing____ in - side.

Would-n't you a - gree, ba - by, you and

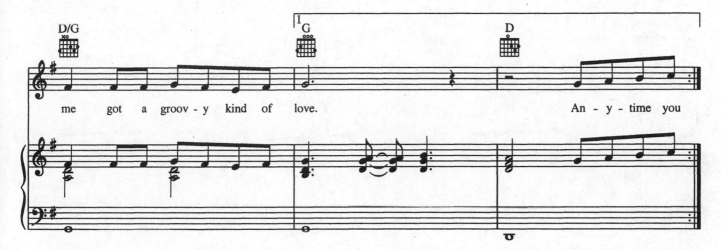

me got a groov - y kind of love.

An - y - time you

love.

Oh. ___

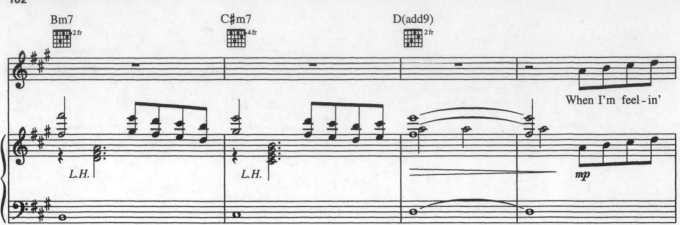

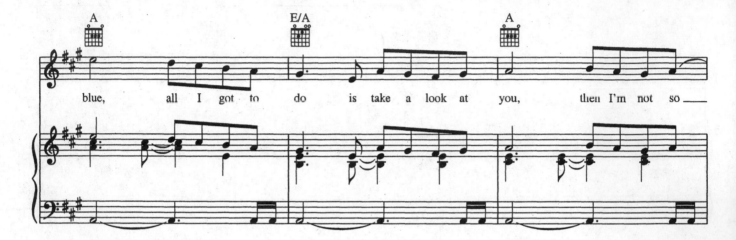

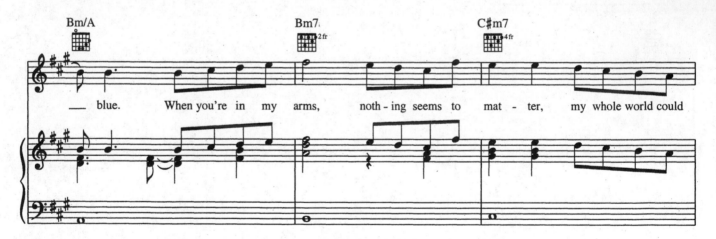

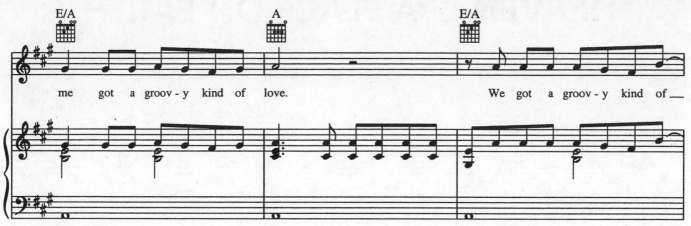

HEAVEN IS A PLACE ON EARTH

Words and Music by RICK NOWELS
and ELLEN SHIPLEY

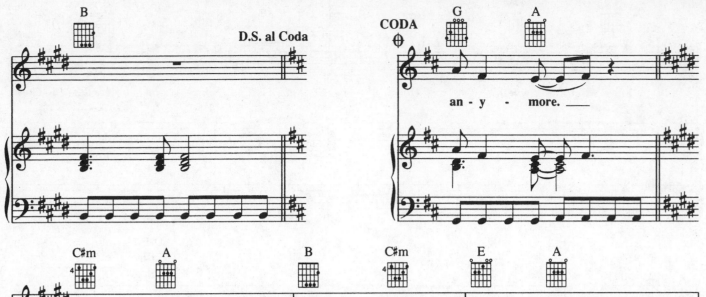

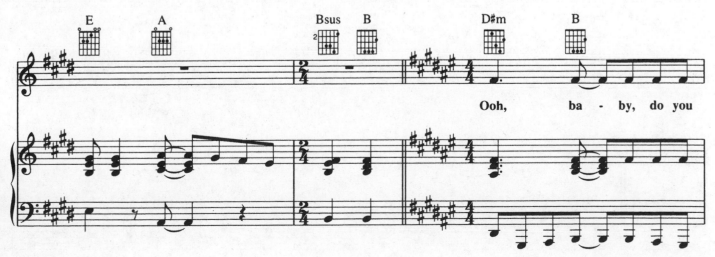

HOW DEEP IS YOUR LOVE

from the Motion Picture SATURDAY NIGHT FEVER

Words and Music by BARRY GIBB,
MAURICE GIBB and ROBIN GIBB

Moderately

I know your eyes in the morn - ing sun. ___ I feel you touch ___
I be - lieve in you. ___ You know the door ___

___ me in the pour - ing rain. ___ And the mo - ment that you wan - der far ___
___ to my ver - y soul. ___ You're the light ___ in my deep - est, dark -

___ from me, I wan - na feel you in my arms a - gain. ___ And you come ___
- est hour; ___ you're my sav - ior when I fall. ___ And you may ___

113

HERE AND NOW

Words and Music by TERRY STEELE
and DAVID ELLIOT

116

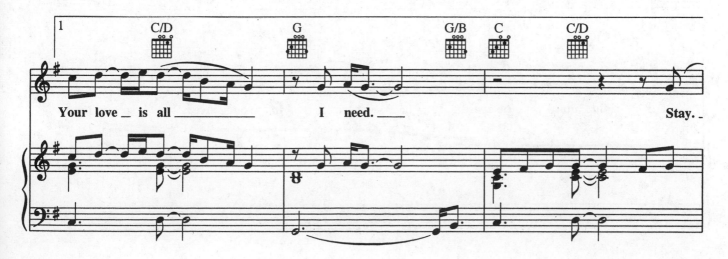

HOW AM I SUPPOSED TO LIVE WITHOUT YOU

Words and Music by MICHAEL BOLTON
and DOUG JAMES

I BELIEVE IN YOU AND ME

from the Touchstone Motion Picture THE PREACHER'S WIFE

Words and Music by DAVID WOLFERT
and SANDY LINZER

I be-lieve in you ___ and me. ___ I be-lieve that

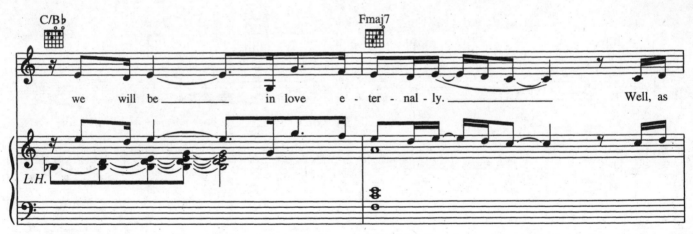

we will be ___ in love e-ter-nal-ly. ___ Well, as

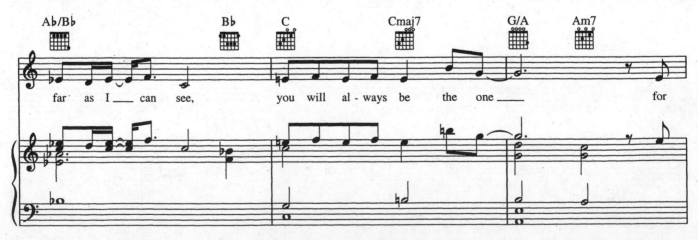

far as I ___ can see, you will al-ways be the one ___ for

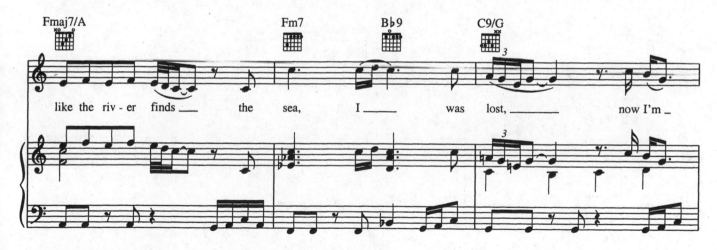

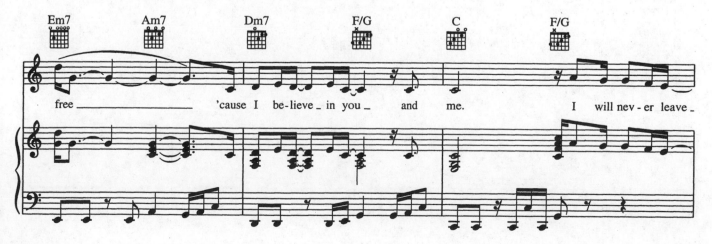

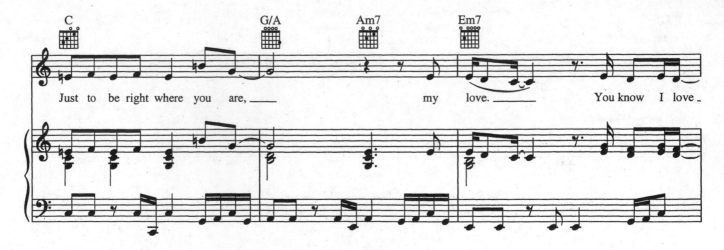

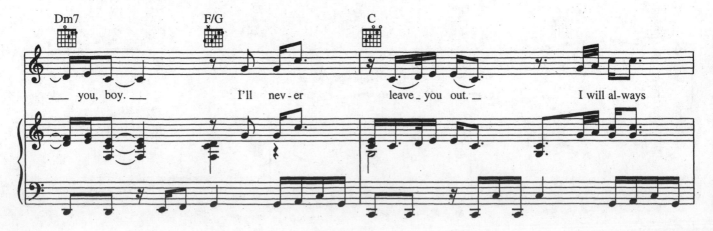

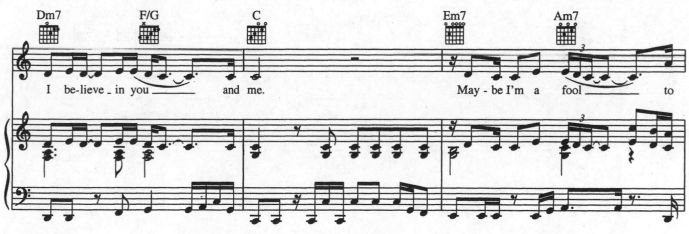

I be-lieve, _ I do be-lieve in you and me. See, I'm _

lost, ___ now I'm free ___ 'cause

I be-lieve in you and _ me. _

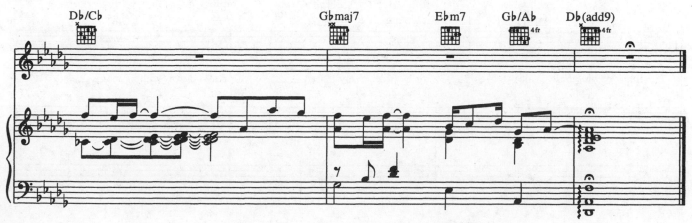

I CAN'T MAKE YOU LOVE ME

Words and Music by MIKE REID
and ALLEN SHAMBLIN

134

you're hold - in' me. _____ Morn - in' will come ___ and I'll do what's right. _ Just

give me till then _____ to give up _____ this fight. _____ And I will give up this fight. _____

'Cause I can't

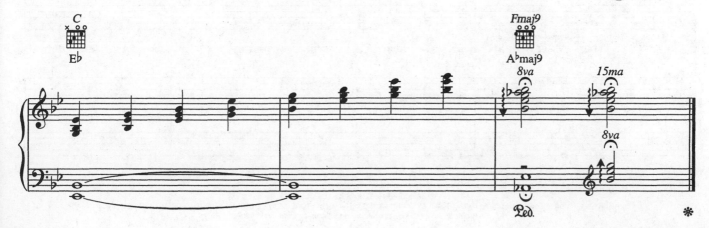

I HEAR A SYMPHONY

Words and Music by EDWARD HOLLAND,
LAMONT DOZIER and BRIAN HOLLAND

You've giv-en me a true love, and ev-'ry day I thank _ you, love,

for a feel-ing that's _ so new, _ so in-vit-ing, so ex-cit-ing.

When-ev-er you are near, I hear a sym-pho-ny, a ten-der

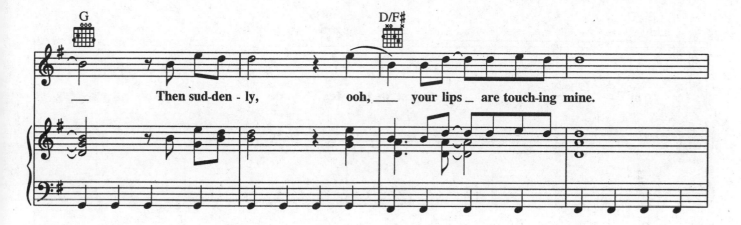

138

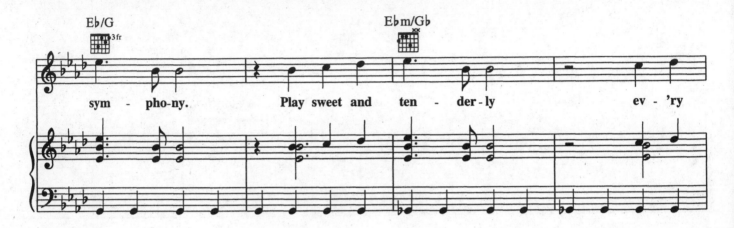

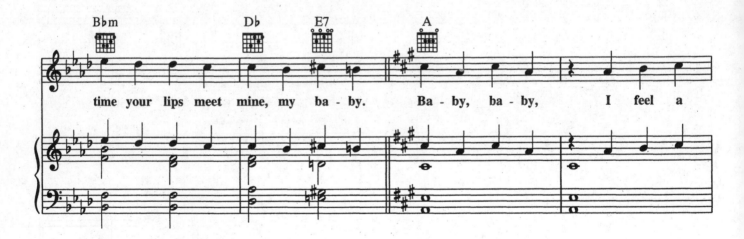

I HONESTLY LOVE YOU

Words and Music by PETER ALLEN
and JEFF BARRY

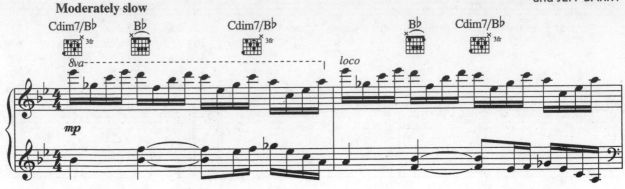

May-be I hang a-round__ here a lit-tle more than I should; we

You don't__ have to an-swer; I see it in your eyes.

both know I got some-where else__ to go. But

May-be it was bet-ter left__ un-said. But

141

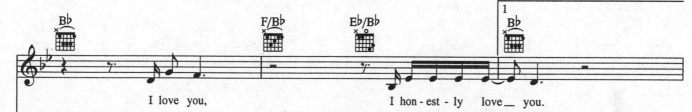

I'm not tryin' to make__ you feel__ un-

com-f'ta-ble.__ I'm not tryin' to make you an-y-thing__ at all. But this

feel-ing does-n't come__ a-long ev-'ry day,__ and you

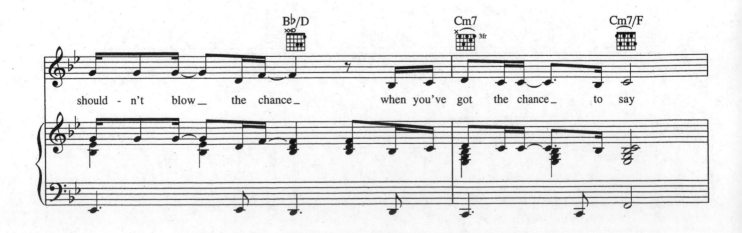

should-n't blow__ the chance__ when you've got the chance__ to say

I love you.   *(Spoken:) I love you.*

I hon-est-ly love __ you.

If we both __ were born __ in an-oth-er place and time, this

mo-ment might be end-ing in a kiss.   But there you are with yours __ and

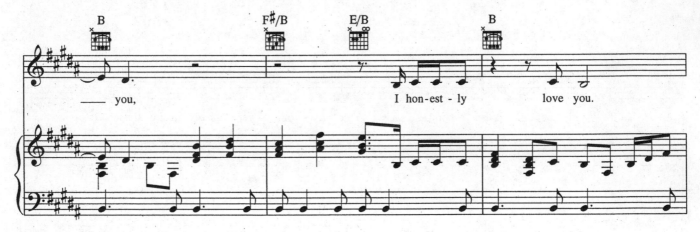

I JUST CALLED TO SAY I LOVE YOU

Words and Music by
STEVIE WONDER

Moderately

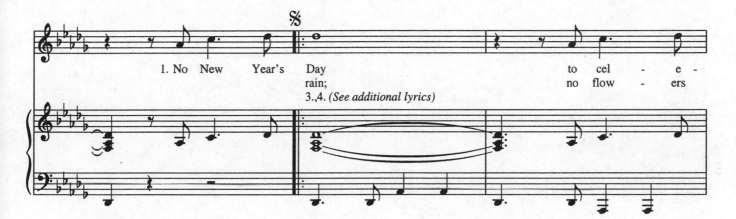

1. No New Year's Day to cel - e -
rain; no flow - ers
3.,4. (See additional lyrics)

brate; no choc - 'late cov - ered can - dy hearts
bloom; no wed - ding Sat - ur - day with - in

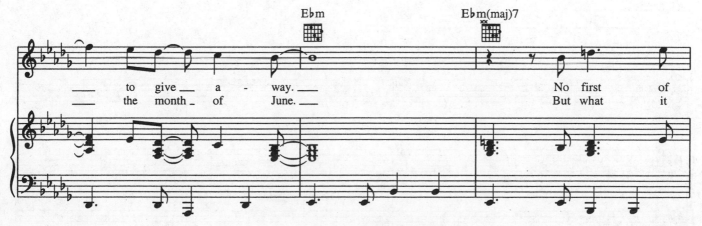

to give a way. No first of
the month of June. But what it

spring; _____ no song to sing.
is _____ is some- thing true,

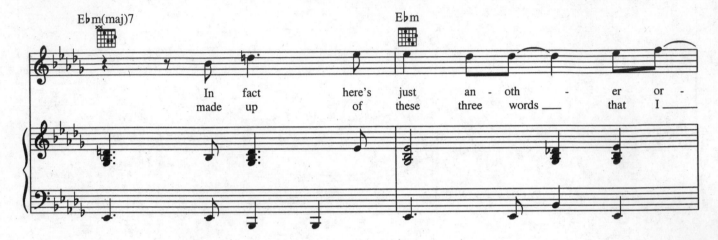

In fact here's just an- oth- er or -
made up of these three words ___ that I ___

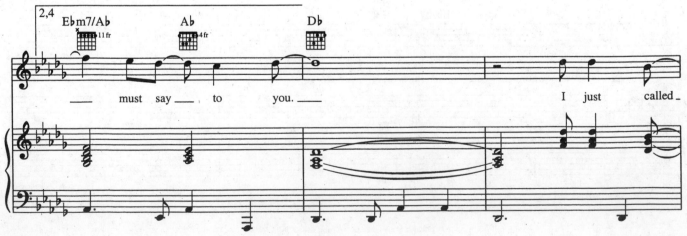

1,3

- di- nar- y day. ___ 2. No A- pril

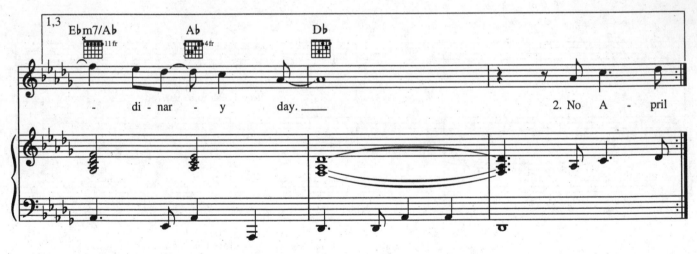

2,4

___ must say ___ to you. ___ I just called ___

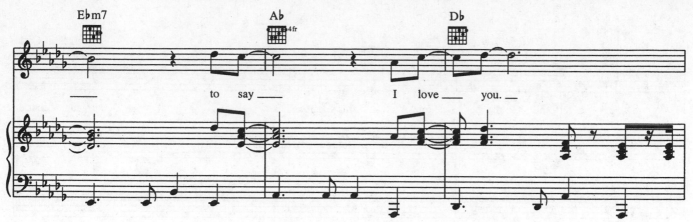

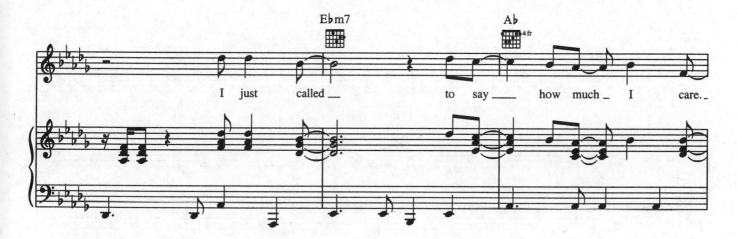

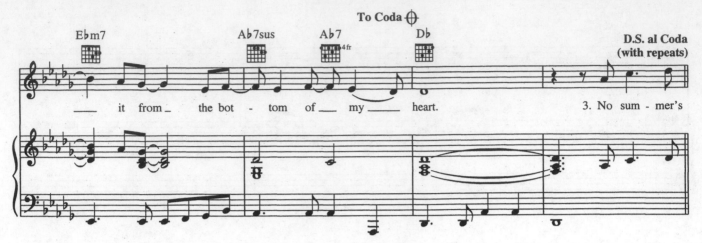

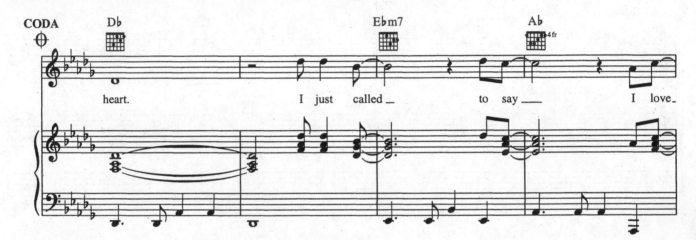

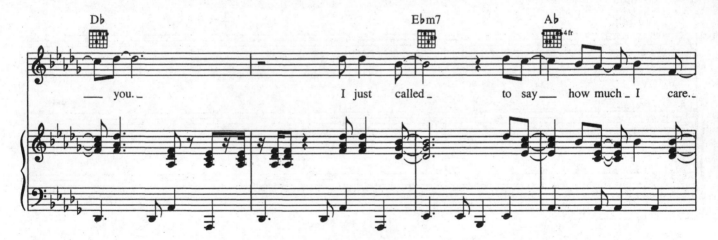

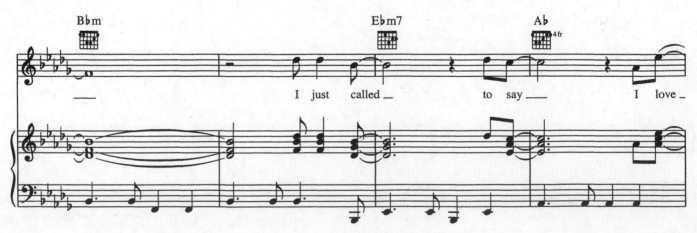

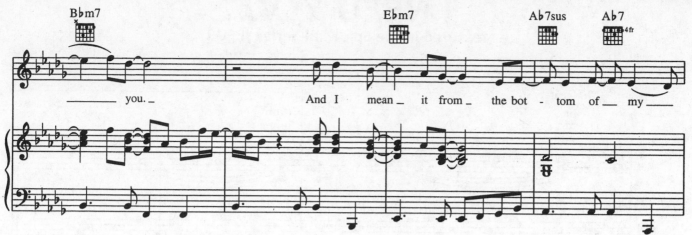

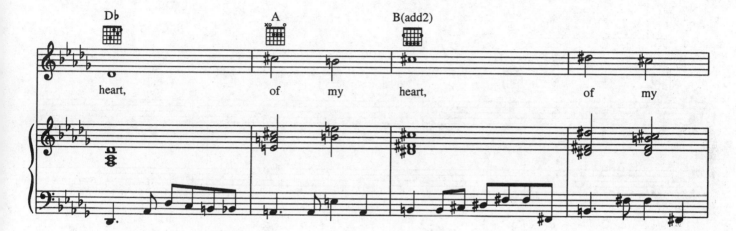

Additional Lyrics

3. No summer's high; no warm July;
   No harvest moon to light one tender August night.
   No autumn breeze; no falling leaves;
   Not even time for birds to fly to southern skies.

4. No Libra sun; no Halloween;
   No giving thanks to all the Christmas joy you bring.
   But what it is, though old so new
   To fill your heart like no three words could ever do.

I NEED YOU

featured in the Epic Mini-Series JESUS

Words and Music by DENNIS MATKOSKY
and TY LACY

I don't need a lot ___ of things;   I can

*Vocal line written one octave higher than sung.

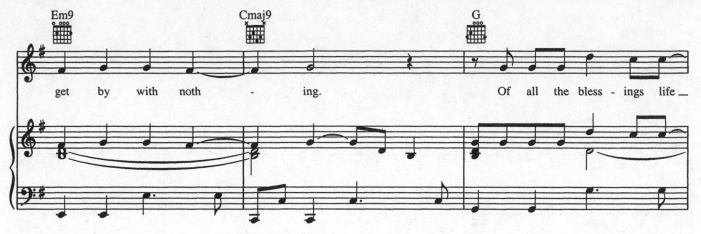

get by with noth - ing. Of all the bless - ings life

___ can bring, I've al - ways need - ed some - thing.

But I've ___ got all ___ I ___ want ___ when it comes to lov - ing You. ___

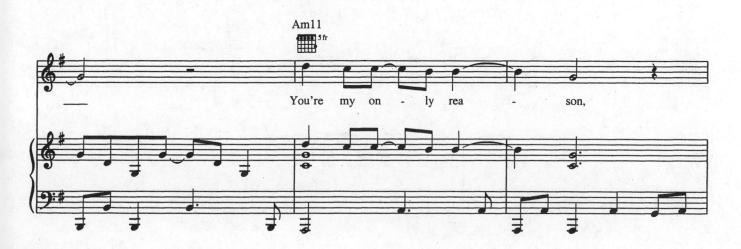

You're my on - ly rea - son,

152

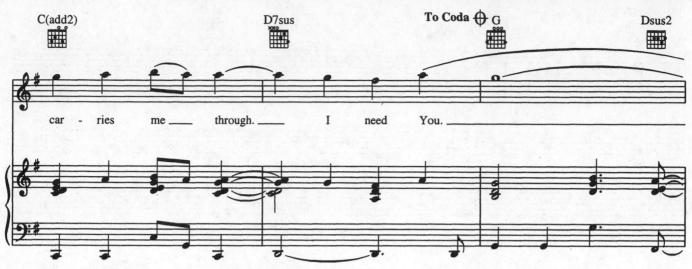

car - ries me ____ through. ____ I need You. _____

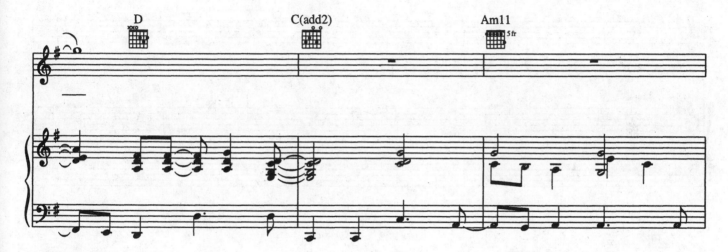

You're the hope that moves ____ me to

156

I WILL

Words and Music by JOHN LENNON
and PAUL McCARTNEY

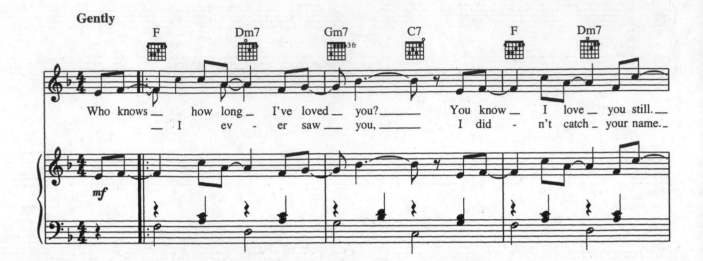

Who knows __ how long __ I've loved __ you? _____ You know __ I love __ you still. ___
__ I ev - er saw __ you, _____ I did - n't catch __ your name. __

__ Will I wait __ a lone - ly life - time? If you want __
__ But it nev - er real - ly mat - tered; I will al -

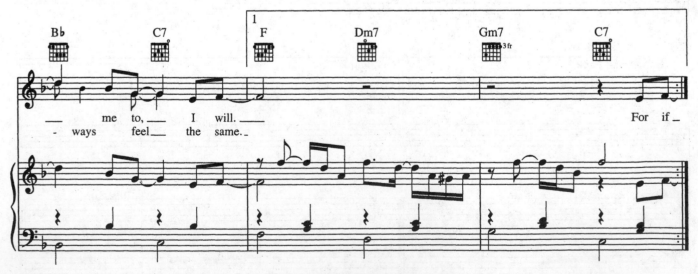

__ me to, __ I will. __ For if
- ways feel __ the same. __

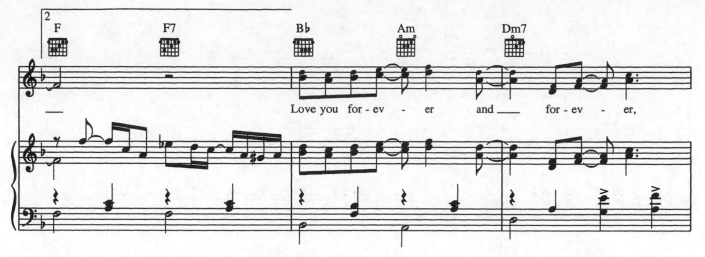

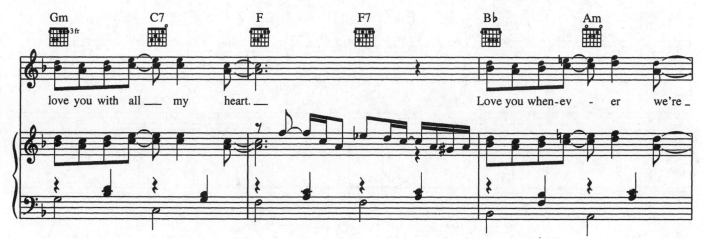

160

I WON'T LAST A DAY WITHOUT YOU

Words and Music by PAUL WILLIAMS
and ROGER NICHOLS

Moderately slow

Day af-ter day___ I must face a world___ of strang-ers where I
So man-y times___ when the cit-y seems___ to be with-out a

don't be-long;___ I'm not that strong. It's nice to know___ that there's
friend-ly face,___ a lone-ly place, it's nice to know___ that you'll

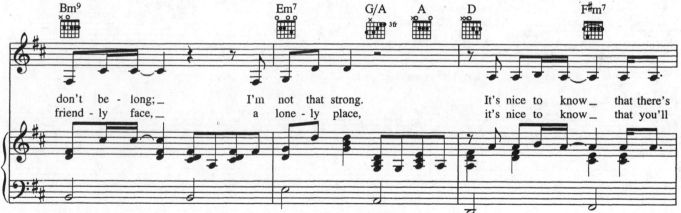

some-one I___ can turn to who will al-ways care;___ you're
be there if___ I need you, and you'll al-ways smile;___ it's

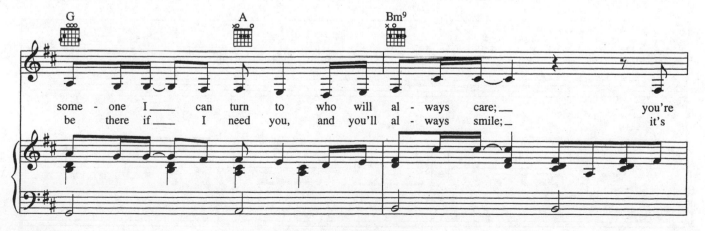

al-ways there. } all worth-while. } When there's no get-ting o-ver that rain-bow,_ when my

small-est of dreams_ won't come_ true, I can take all the mad-ness the

world_ has to give,_ but I won't_ last a day_ with-out you._

I WILL BE HERE

Words and Music by
STEVEN CURTIS CHAPMAN

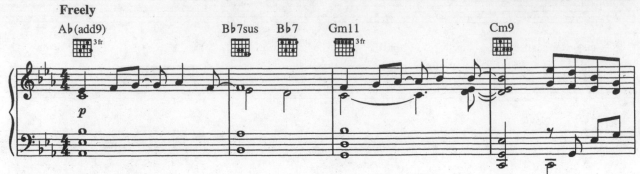

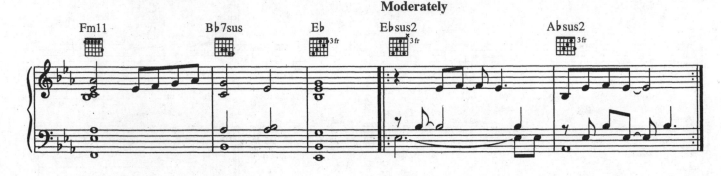

To-mor-row morn-in' if you __ wake up and the sun does not __ ap-pear,

To-mor-row morn-in' if you __ wake up and the fu-ture is __ un-clear,

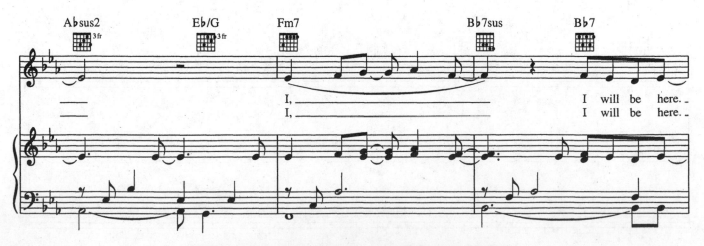

__ I, _____ I will be here.

__ I, _____ I will be here.

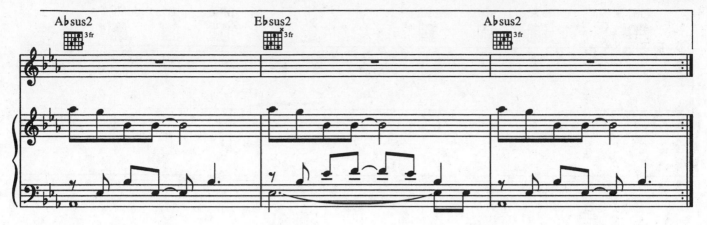

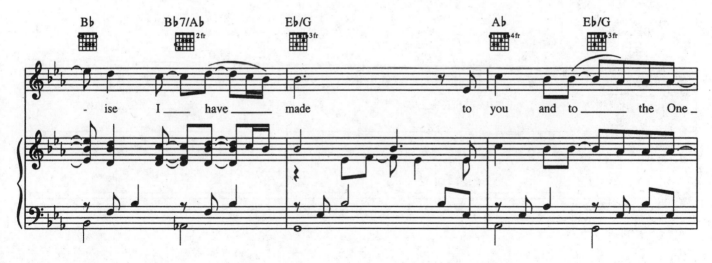

Hmm, _____ I will __ be __ true to the prom -

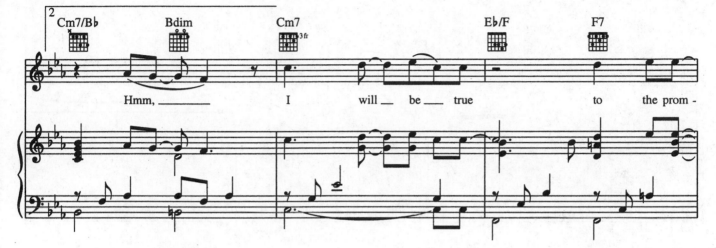

- ise I __ have __ made to you and to ____ the One __

__ who gave you to _____ me.

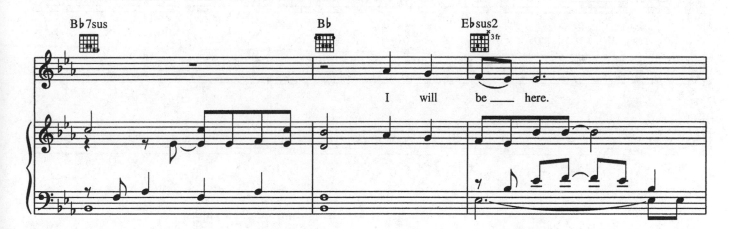

I'D DO ANYTHING FOR LOVE
(But I Won't Do That)

Words and Music by
JIM STEINMAN

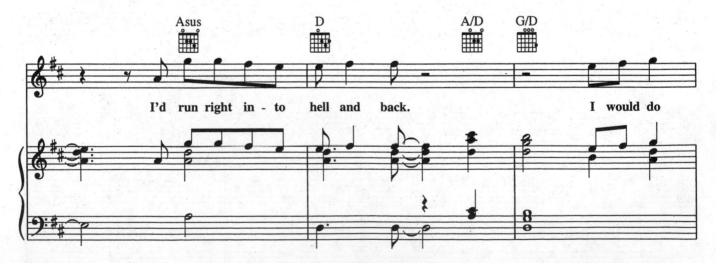

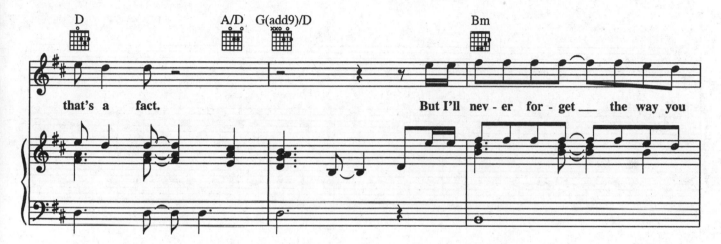

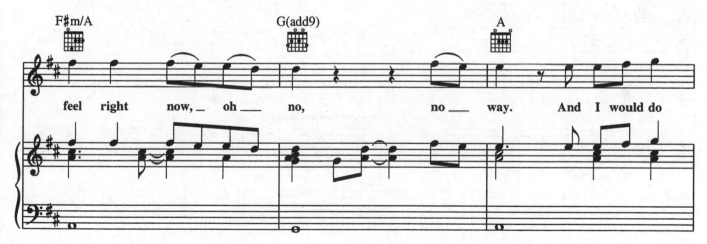

174

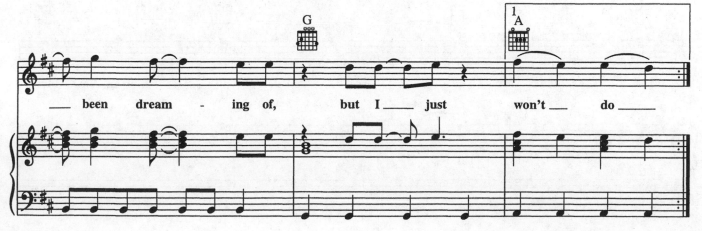

I'LL BE THERE

Words and Music by BERRY GORDY, HAL DAVIS,
WILLIE HUTCH and BOB WEST

Bb/C
F
C/E
holding on.
Let me fill your heart with joy and laughter.
Dm
Dm/C
Am7
Bb
Gm7
Togetherness, well it's all I'm after.
Just call my
3
Bb/C
F
C7sus
D.S. al Coda
name and I'll be there.
(I'll be there.)
CODA
Bb/C
holding on.
3

I'LL BE LOVING YOU
(Forever)

Words and Music by
MAURICE STARR

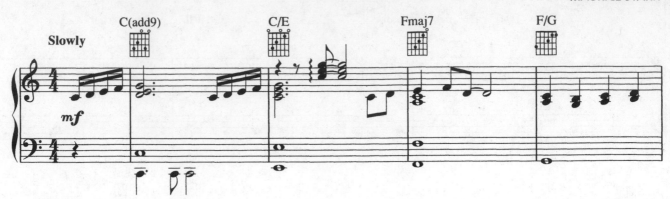

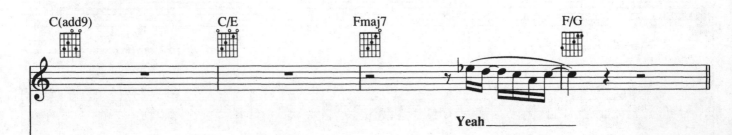

Yeah _____

I'm not that kind of guy ___ who can take a bro - ken heart, ___ so don't
I count the bless - ings ___ that keep our love new. ___ There's

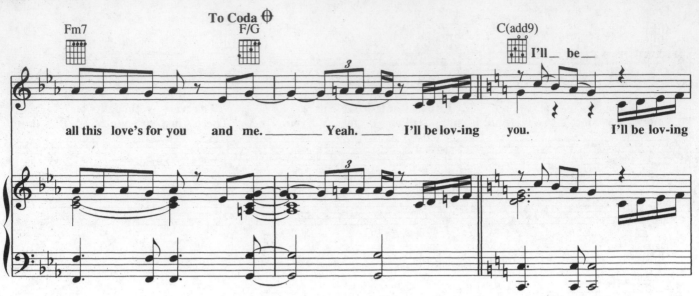

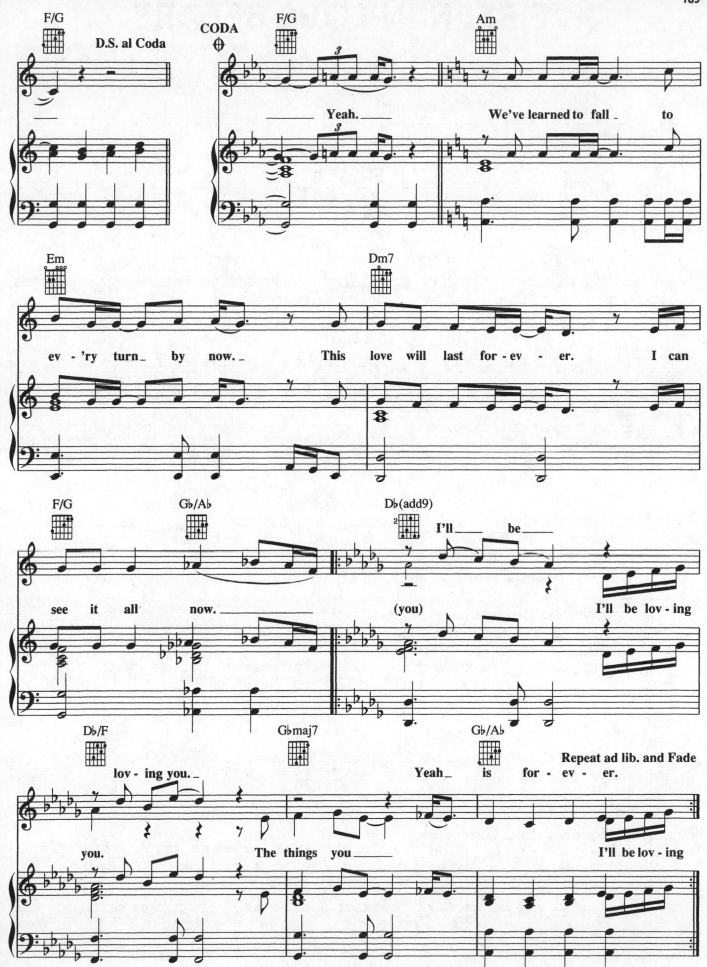

I'VE BEEN IN LOVE BEFORE

Words and Music by
NICHOLAS EEDE

I've been in love _ be - fore, ___ I've been in love _ be -

fore.

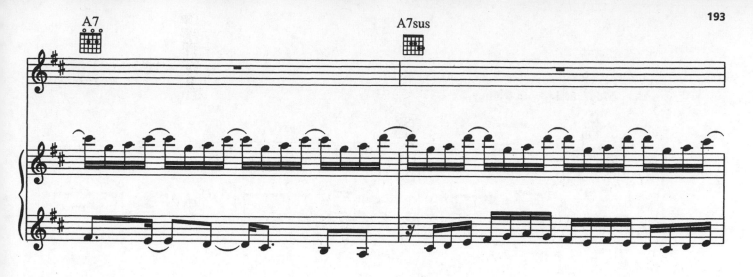

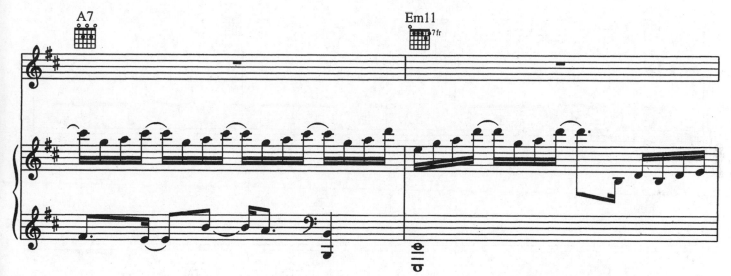

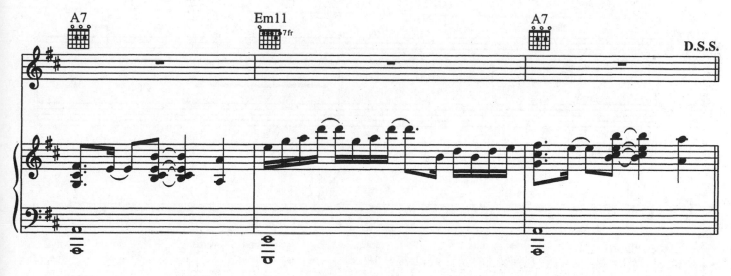

Additional Lyrics

2. **Just one touch, just one look,**
   A dangerous dance.
   One small word can make me feel
   Like running away.
   You can't say you're in it, no,
   Until you reach the limit.
   To Chorus

IF

Words and Music by
DAVID GATES

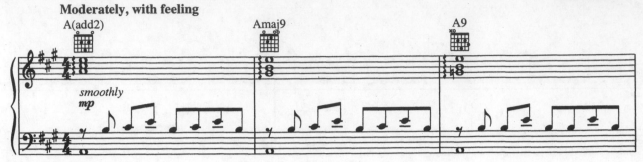

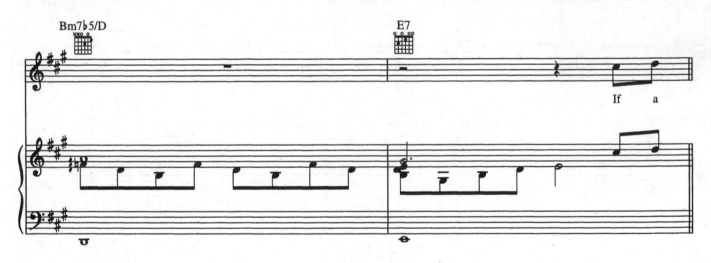

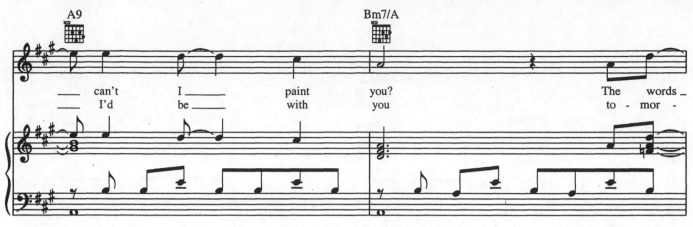

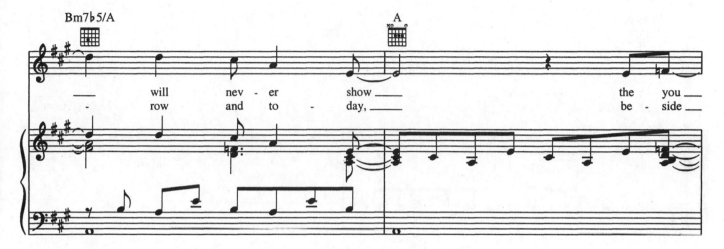

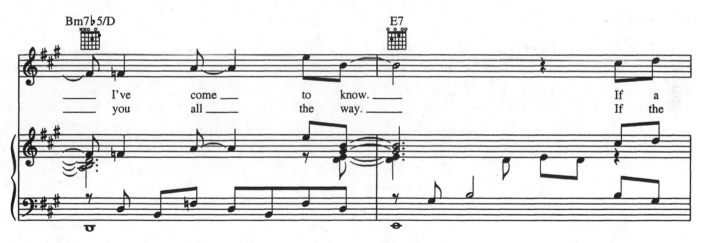

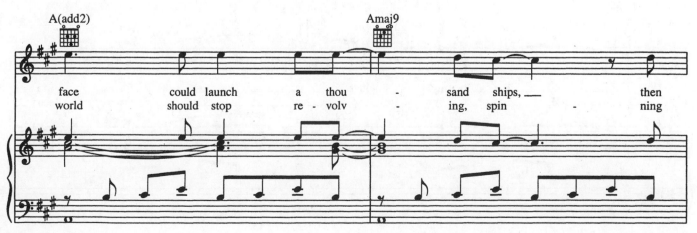

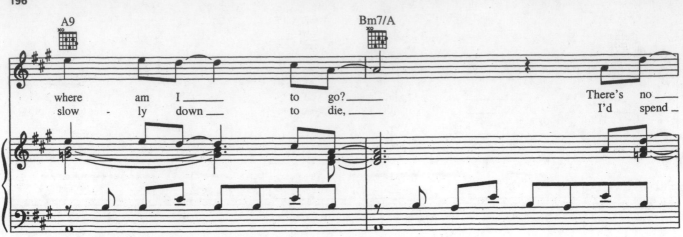

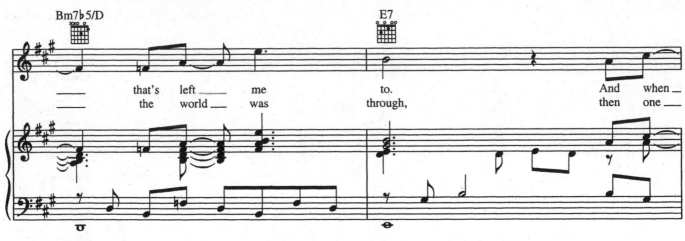

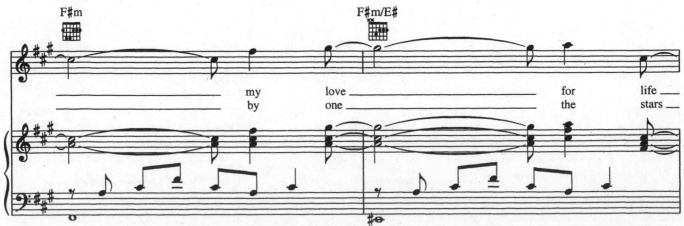

IT'S YOUR LOVE

Words and Music by
STEPHONY E. SMITH

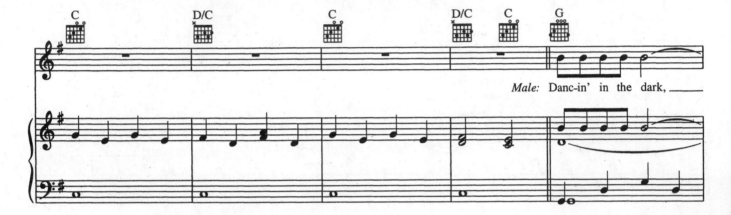

touch-in' my skin, and ask-in' you to do what

you've been do-in' all o-ver a-gain. Oh, it's a beau-ti-ful ___ thing. ___

___ Don't think I can keep it all ___ in. _____ I just got-ta let you know

what it is that ___ won't let me go. *Both:* It's your love. _____ It just does some-thin'

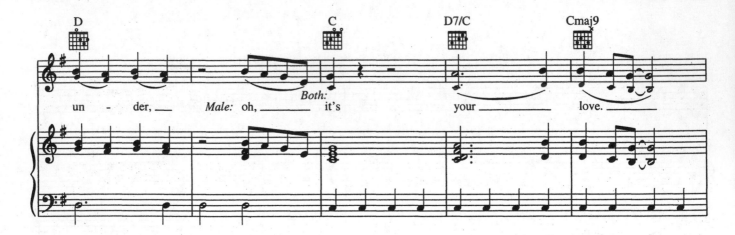

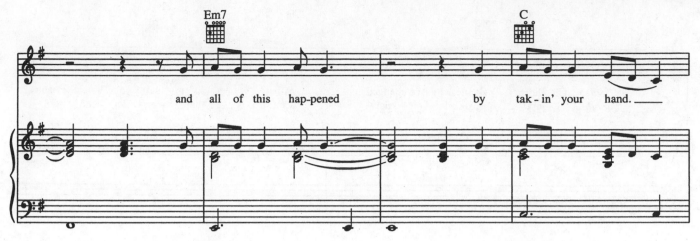

and all of this hap-pened by tak-in' your hand.

And who I am now is who I want-ed to be.

Both: And now that we're to-geth-er, I'm strong-er than ev-er. I'm hap-py and free.

Oh, it's a beau-ti-ful thing. Don't think I can keep it all in.

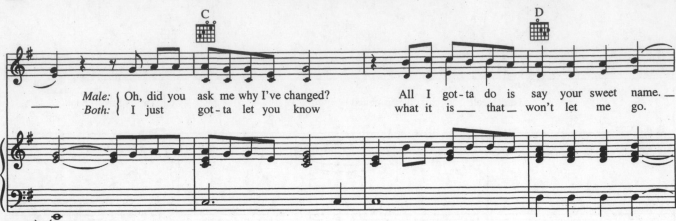

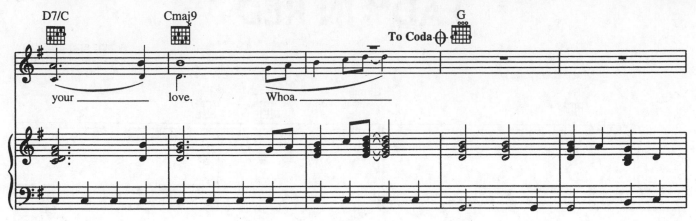

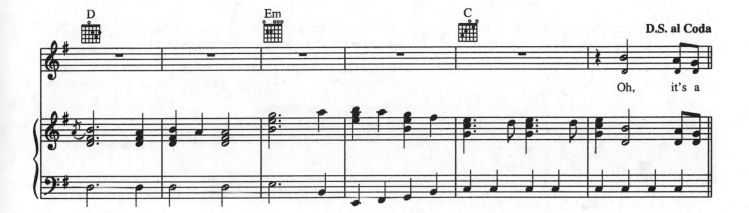

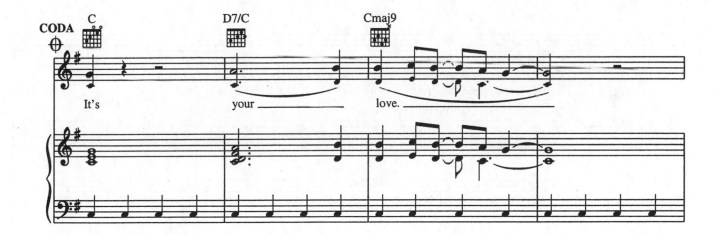

LADY IN RED

Words and Music by
CHRIS DeBURGH

LONGER

Words and Music by
DAN FOGELBERG

Moderate Ballad

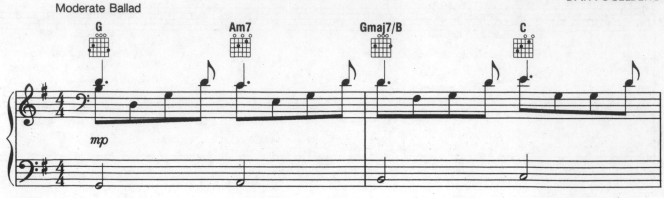

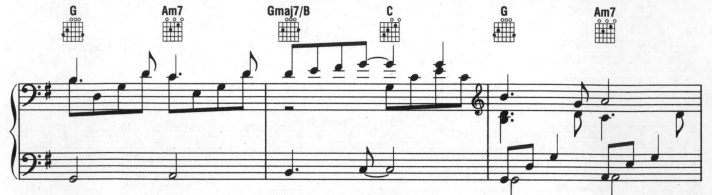

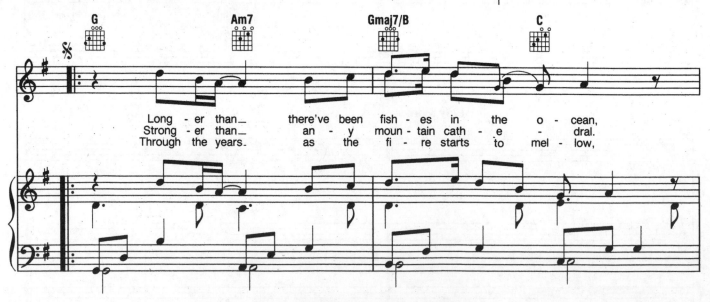

Long - er than___ there've been fish - es in the o - cean,
Strong - er than___ an - y moun - tain cath - e - dral.
Through the years___ as the fi - re starts to mel - low,

high - er than___ an - y bird ev - er flew,___
tru - er than___ an - y tree ev - er grew,___
burn - ing lines___ in the book of our lives.___

Though the

Long - er than___ there've been stars up in the hea - vens,___
Deep - er than___ an - y for - est prim - e - val,___
bind - ing cracks___ and the pag - es start to yel - low,___

I've been in love___ with you.___
I am in love___ with you.
I'll be in love___ with you.

MAKE IT WITH YOU

Words and Music by
DAVID GATES

Life,_____ it's for us to_____ keep. ___
Love_____ can be right or_____ wrong. ___
Life,_____ it's for us to_____ keep. ___

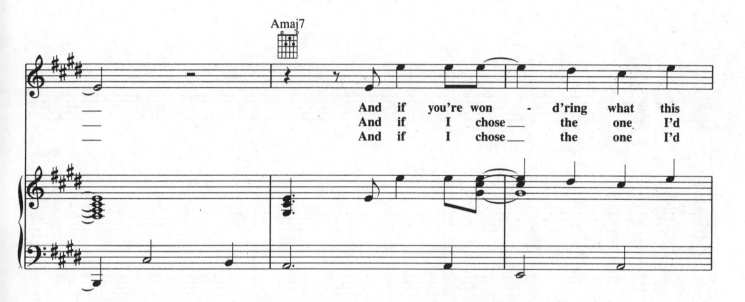

And if you're won - d'ring what this
And if I chose___ the what one I'd
And if I chose___ the one I'd

all is lead - ing to, _____
like to help me through, _____
like to help me through, _____

I want to make___ it with you.___
I'd like to make___ it with you.___
I'd like to make___ it with you.___

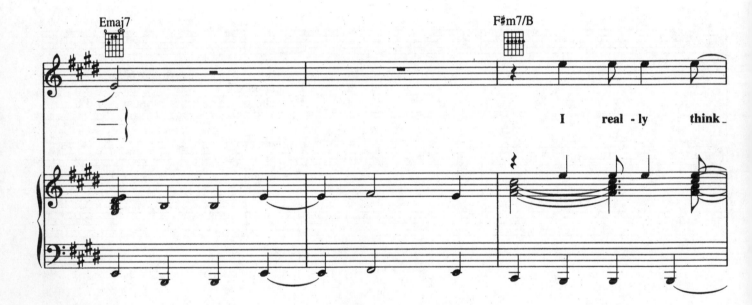

I real - ly think___

that we___ could make___ it, girl.___

LOVE OF MY LIFE

Words and Music by JIM BRICKMAN
and TOM DOUGLAS

LOVE TAKES TIME

Words and Music by MARIAH CAREY
and BEN MARGULIES

223

MY CHERIE AMOUR

Words and Music by STEVIE WONDER,
SYLVIA MOY and HENRY COSBY

227

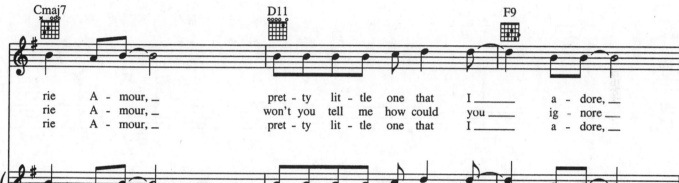

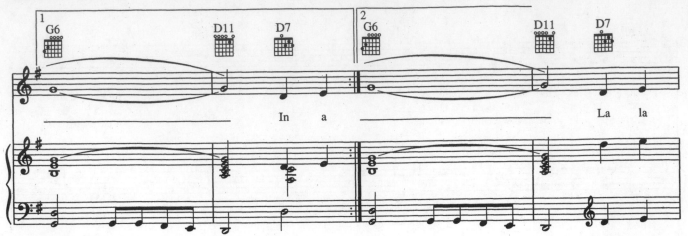

In a _____ La la

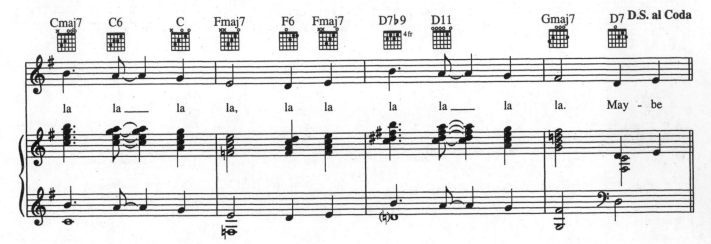

la la ____ la la, la la la la ____ la la. May - be

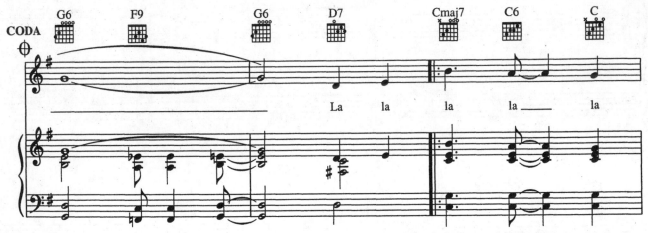

La la la la ____ la

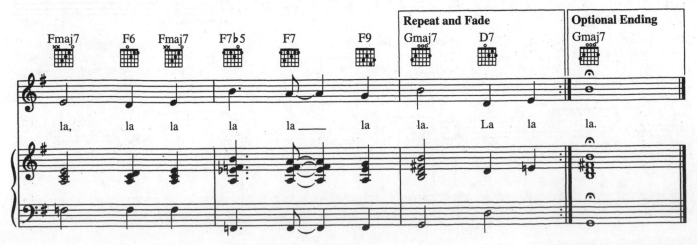

la, la la la la ____ la la. La la la.

MY GIRL

Words and Music by WILLIAM "SMOKEY" ROBINSON
and RONALD WHITE

230

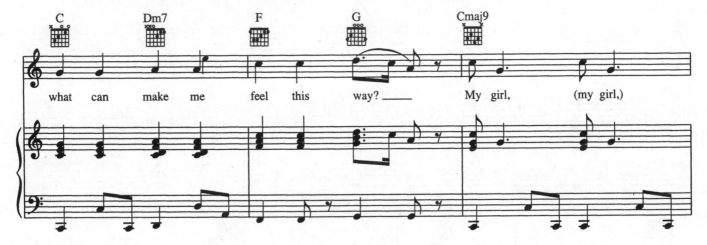

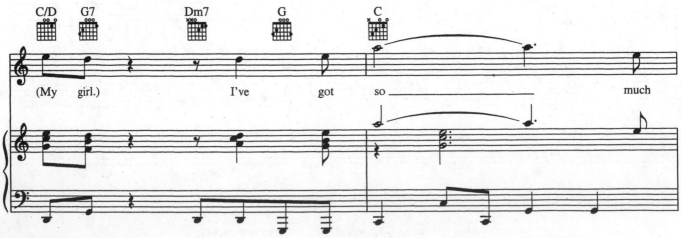

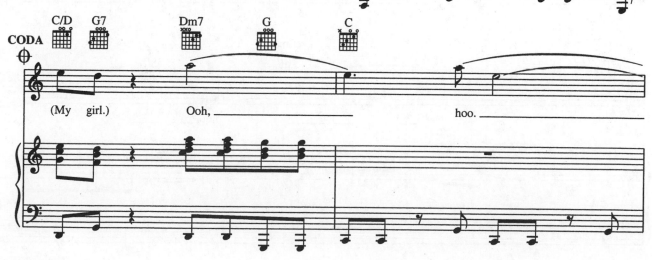

(Hey, hey,   hey.)

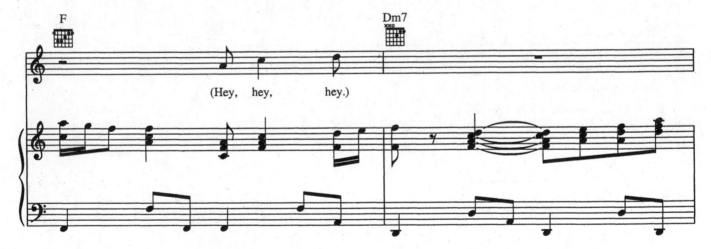

(Hey,   hey,   hey.)

Ooh, _____   hoo, _____   yeah. ___

I don't need no ____ mon - ey, ____

for - tune, or fame. ____

I've got all ____ the rich - es, ba - by,

one man can claim. ____ Well, __

(You Make Me Feel Like)
A NATURAL WOMAN

Words and Music by GERRY GOFFIN,
CAROLE KING and JERRY WEXLER

NEVER CAN SAY GOODBYE

Words and Music by
CLIFTON DAVIS

241

SAVING ALL MY LOVE FOR YOU

Words by GERRY GOFFIN
Music by MICHAEL MASSER

A few __ sto-len mo-ments __ is all __ that we share.
not __ ver-y eas-y __ liv-ing all a-lone. My

You've __ got your fam-'ly __ and they __ need you there. Though I try __ to re-sist, __ be-ing
friends __ try and tell me __ find a man __ of my own. __ But __ each __ time I try, __ I just

last __ on your list, but no oth-er man's __ gon-na do, __ so I'm
break __ down and cry 'cause I'd rath-er be home __ feel-in' blue, __ so I'm

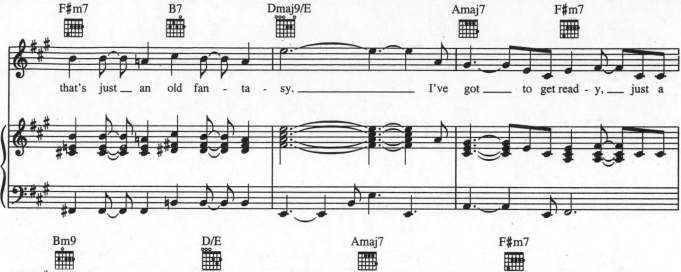

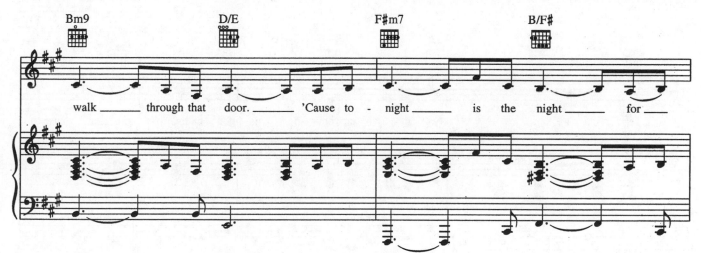

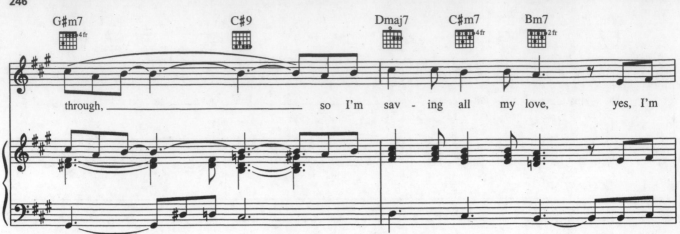

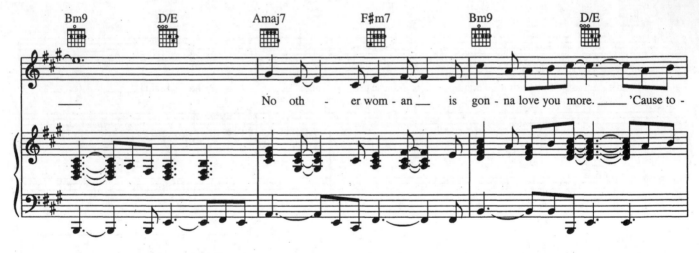

OPERATOR
(That's Not the Way It Feels)

Words and Music by
JIM CROCE

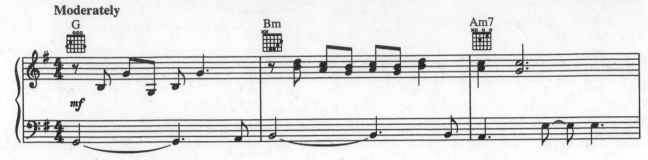

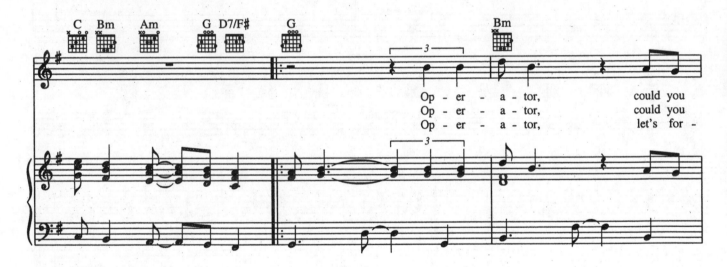

Op - er - a - tor,   could you
Op - er - a - tor,   could you
Op - er - a - tor,   let's for -

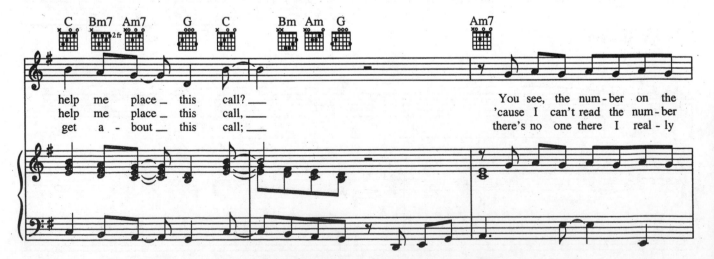

help me place _ this call? _
help me place _ this call, _
get a - bout _ this call; _

You see, the num - ber on the
'cause I can't read the num - ber
there's no one there I real - ly

249

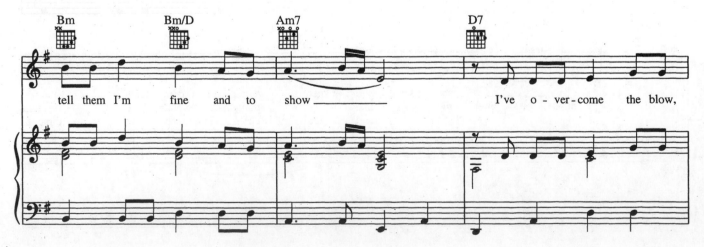

I've learned to take it well.___ I on-ly wish my words___ could just con-vince my-self___

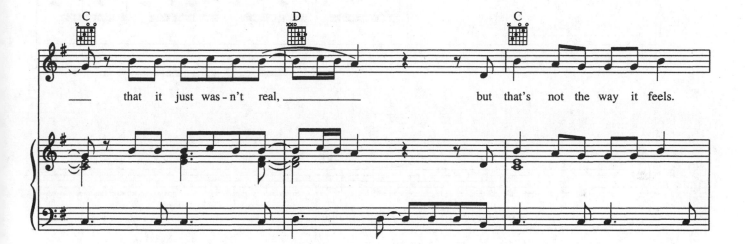

___ that it just was-n't real,_____ but that's not the way it feels.

THE POWER OF LOVE

Words by MARY SUSAN APPLEGATE and JENNIFER RUSH
Music by CANDY DEROUGE and GUNTHER MENDE

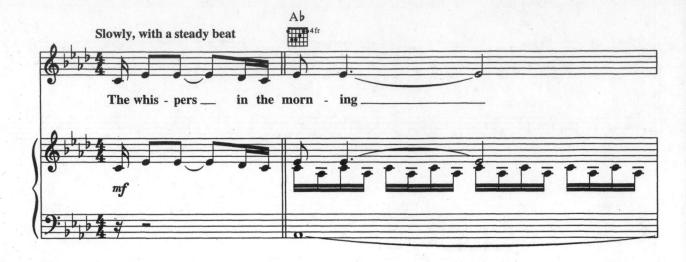

Slowly, with a steady beat

The whis - pers ___ in the morn - ing ___

of lov-ers sleep - ing tight

are roll - ing by ___ like thun - der now,

253

The sound of your heart beat - ing _____ made it clear sud - den - ly.

The feel - ing that I can't go__ on _____

is light years a - way. _____ 'Cause I'm your la -

-ened but I'm read-y to learn ___ 'bout the pow-er of love..

The pow-er of ___ love. _____

Repeat and Fade

PRECIOUS AND FEW

Words and Music by
WALTER D. NIMS

259

261

RIBBON IN THE SKY

Words and Music by
STEVIE WONDER

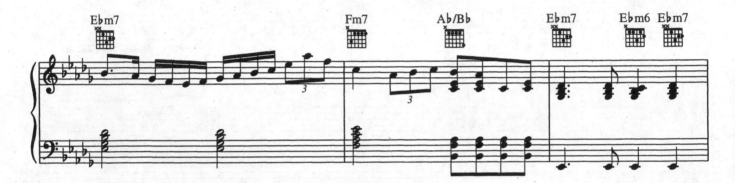

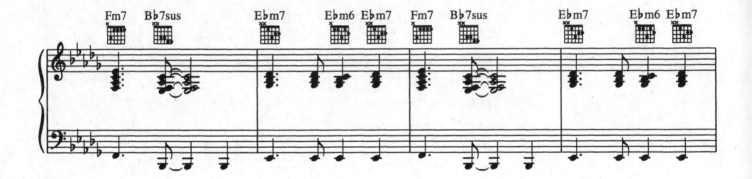

Oh, so

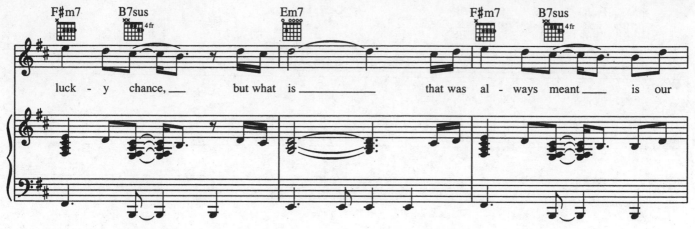

luck - y chance, ___ but what is ___ that was al - ways meant ___ is our

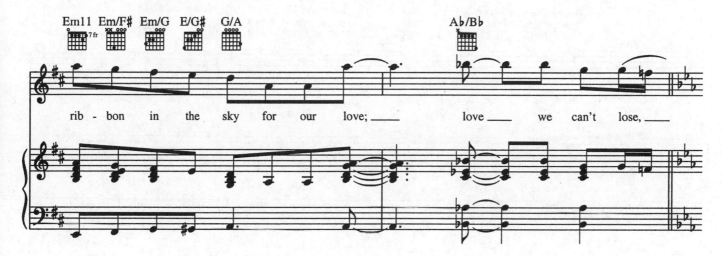

rib - bon in the sky for our love; ___ love ___ we can't lose, ___

___ with God on our side. ___ We'll find strength ___ in each

tear we cry. ___ From now on ___ it will be you and I ___ and our

SAVE THE BEST FOR LAST

Words and Music by PHIL GALDSTON,
JON LIND and WENDY WALDMAN

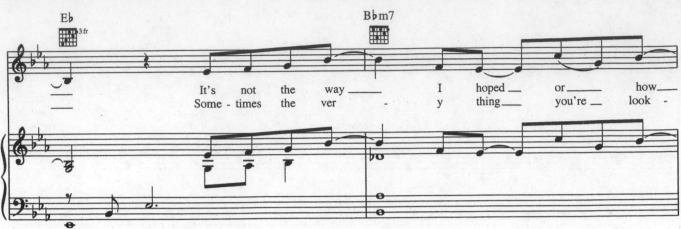

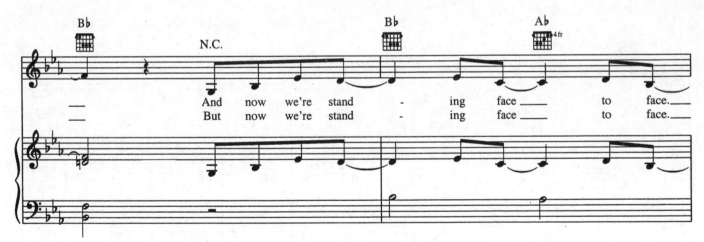

Just when I thought our chance had passed,

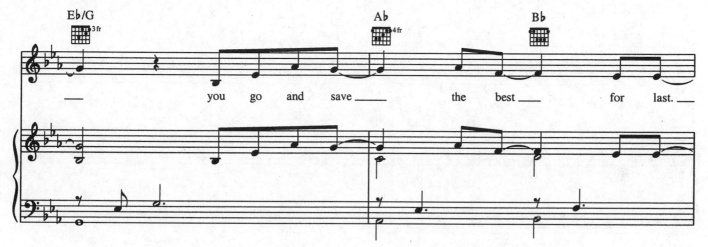

you go and save the best for last.

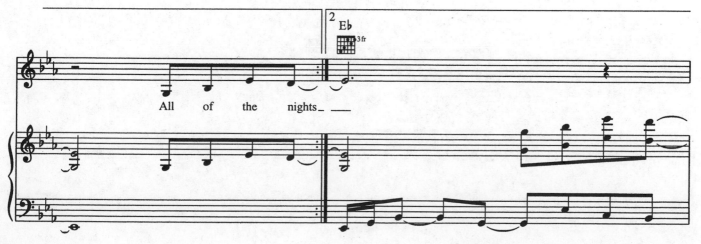

All of the nights

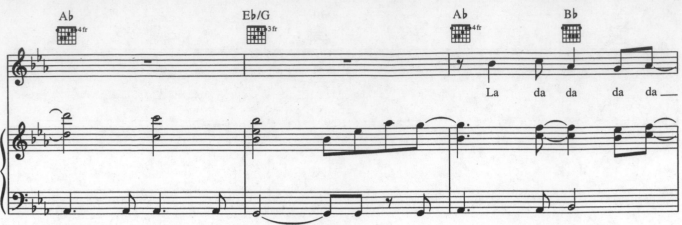

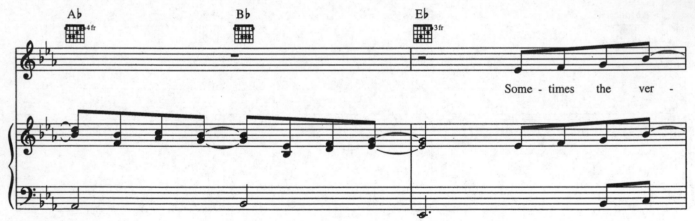

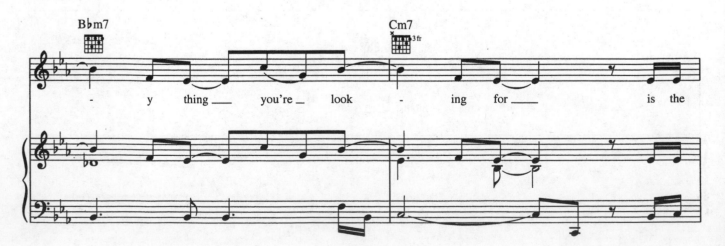

one thing you can't see. Some-times the snow

You went and saved the best for last.

Yeah.

SO FAR AWAY

Words and Music by
CAROLE KING

so man - y dreams __ I've yet to find. _____ But you're so

far   a - way!   Does-n't   an - y - bod - y   stay   in   one   place __
time   a - way.   Long   a - go,   I   reached   for   you   and __

____   an - y - more? __   It   would   be   so   fine   to   see __ your __
____   there   you __ stood.   Hold - ing   you   a - gain   could   on - ly __

Repeat and Fade

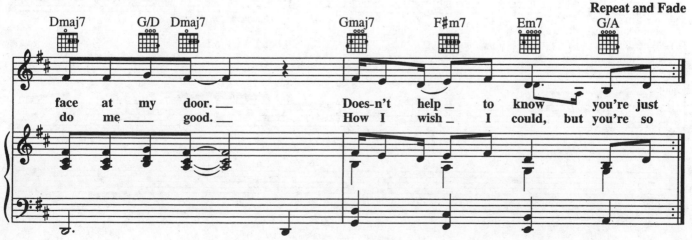

face   at   my   door. __   Does-n't   help __ to   know _____ you're   just
do   me _____ good. __   How   I   wish __ I   could,   but   you're   so

SOMETHING

Words and Music by
GEORGE HARRISON

SOMETIMES WHEN WE TOUCH

Words by DAN HILL
Music by BARRY MANN

Slowly, in 2

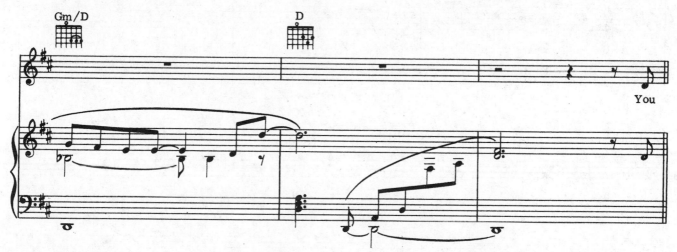

ask me if___ I love___ you,___ and I choke on my___ re-ply.___
mance and all___ its strat-e-gy leaves me bat-tling with___ my pride.___
times I un-der-stand___ you,___ and I know how hard___ you've tried.___

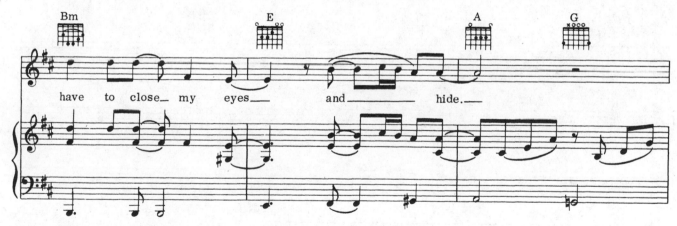

both break down and cry. I wan-na

hold you till the fear in me sub-

To Coda

1. sides.

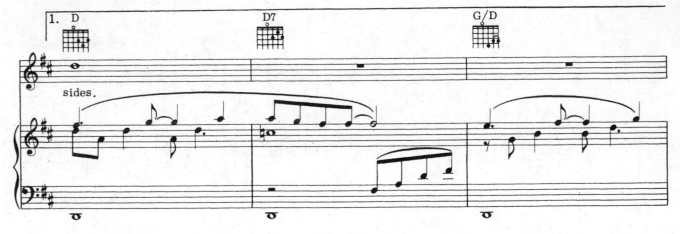

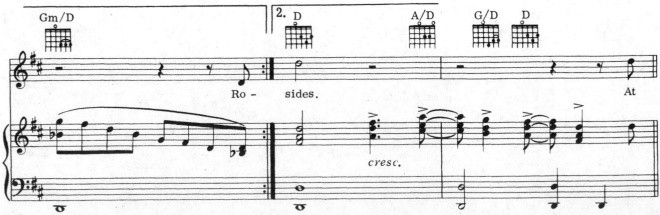

Ro - sides. At

cresc.

SOMETHING ABOUT
THE WAY YOU LOOK TONIGHT

Words and Music by ELTON JOHN
and BERNIE TAUPIN

Original key: F♯ major. This edition has been transposed down one half-step to be more playable.

I was feel - ing like __ a cloud __ a - cross the sun. __
you just shine like __ a bea - con of the bay. __
I'm speech - less and __ I don't know where to start. __

Well, I need to

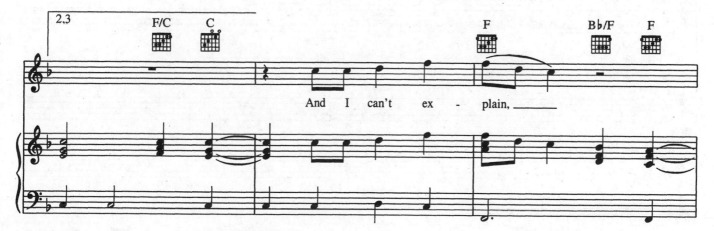

And I can't ex - plain, _____

but there's some-thing a - bout __ the way __ you

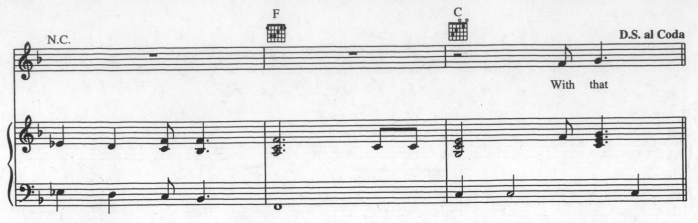

N.C.

F

C

D.S. al Coda

With that

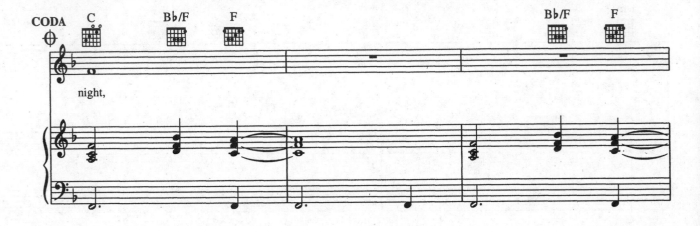

CODA

C

Bb/F

F

Bb/F

F

night,

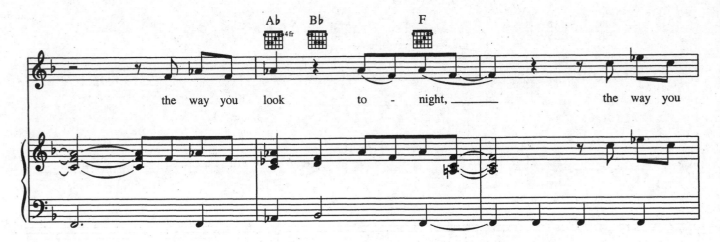

Ab

Bb

F

the way you look to - night, _____ the way you

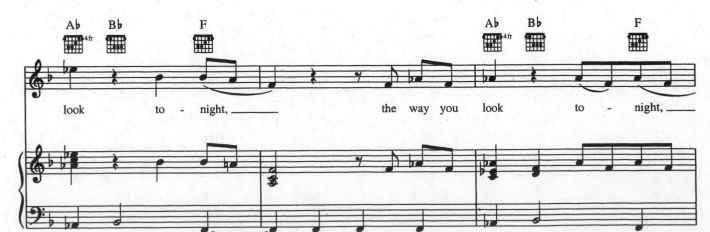

Ab

Bb

F

Ab

Bb

F

look to - night, _____ the way you look to - night, _____

STILL

Words and Music by
LIONEL RICHIE

Slowly (♩ = 66)

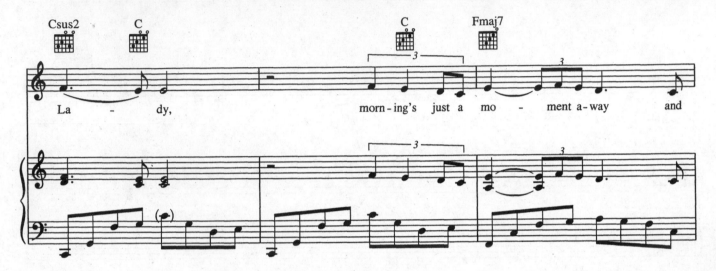

La - dy, morn - ing's just a mo - ment a-way and

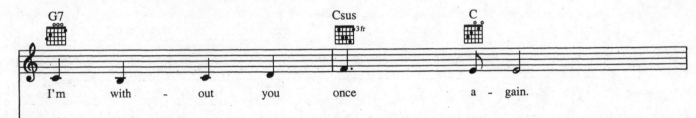

I'm with - out you once a - gain.

You laughed at me,

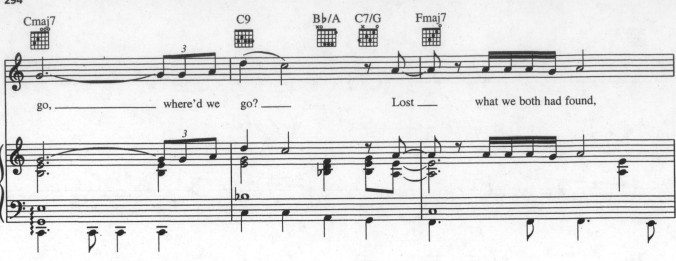

go, _____ where'd we go? _____ Lost _____ what we both had found,

you know we let _____ each oth - er down.

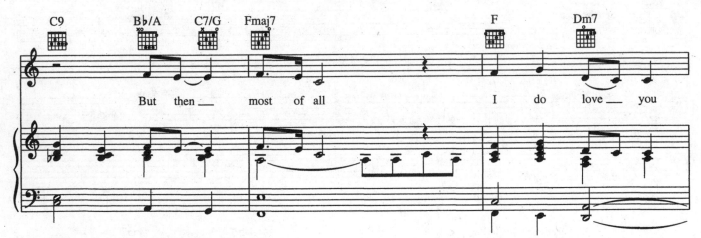

But then ___ most of all I do love ___ you

(whisper) still.

THAT'S WHAT LOVE IS ALL ABOUT

Words and Music by MICHAEL BOLTON
and ERIC KAZ

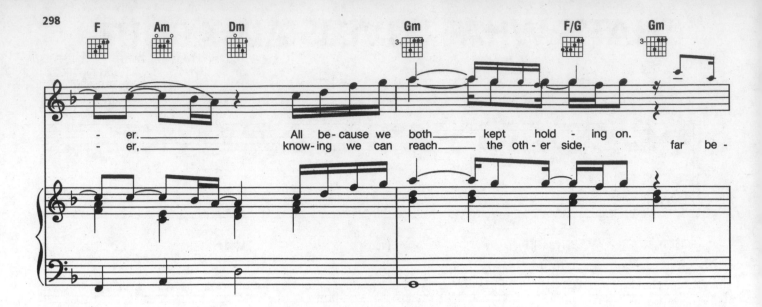

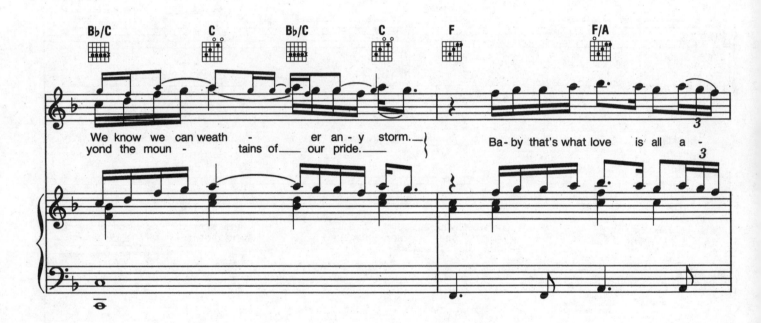

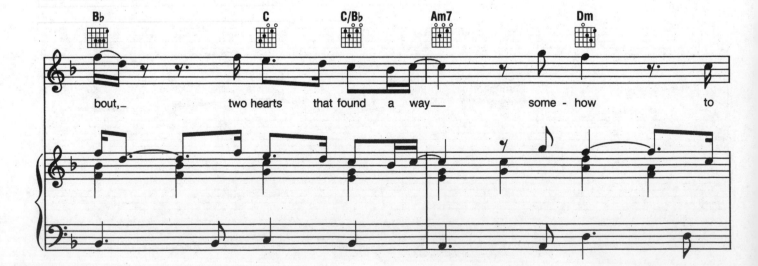

THERE'S A KIND OF HUSH
(All Over the World)

Words and Music by LES REED
and GEOFF STEPHENS

THREE TIMES A LADY

Words and Music by
LIONEL RICHIE

When we are to - geth - er, the

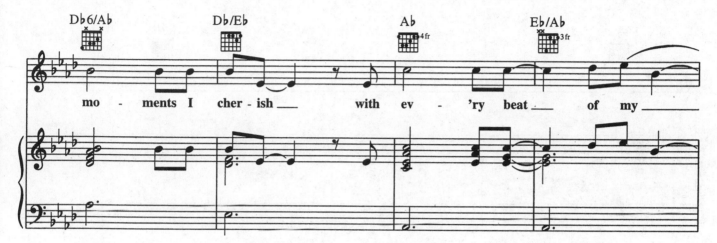

mo - ments I cher - ish ___ with ev - 'ry beat ___ of my ___

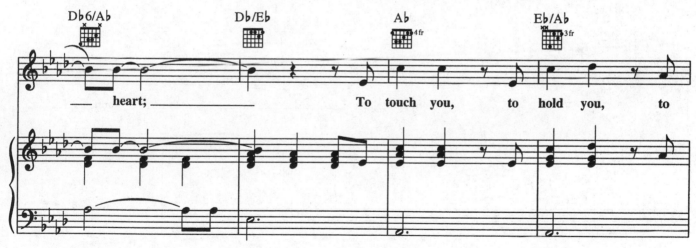

___ heart; _____ To touch you, to hold you, to

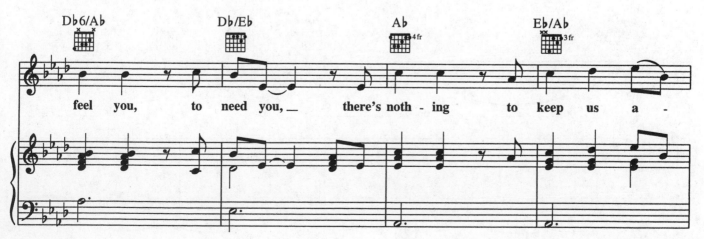

feel you, to need you, ___ there's noth - ing to keep us a -

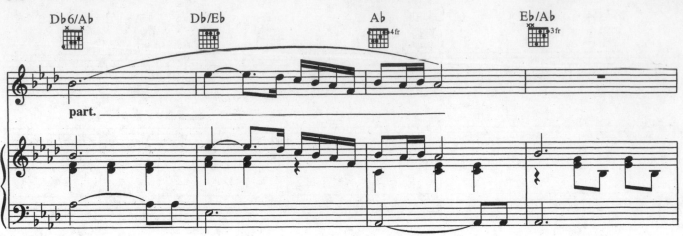

With pedal

TIME IN A BOTTLE

Words and Music by
JIM CROCE

If I could save time in a bottle, _____
I could make days last for - ev - er, _____

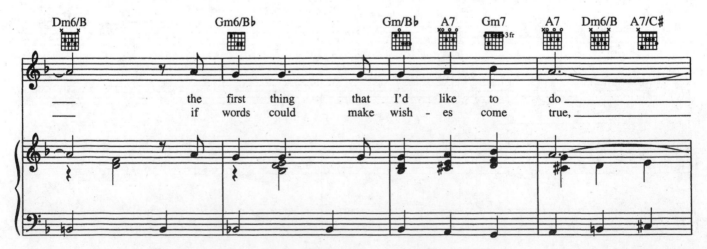

the first thing that I'd like to do _____
if words could make wish - es to come true, _____

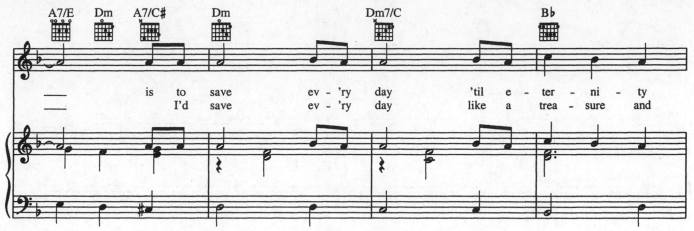

is to save ev-'ry day 'til e - ter - ni - ty

I'd save ev-'ry day like a trea - sure and

pass - es a - way just to spend them with you.

then a - gain I would spend them with you.

If ___ But there nev - er seems to

be e - nough time to do the things you want to do once you

find them. _____ I've

looked a-round e-nough to know that you're the one I want to go through

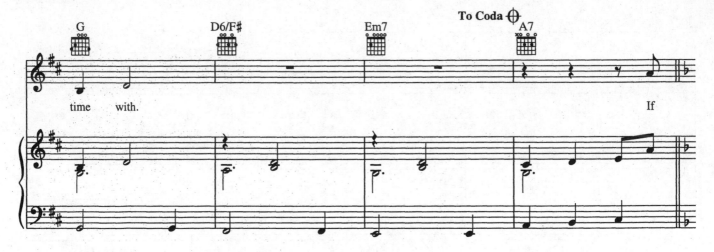

time with. If

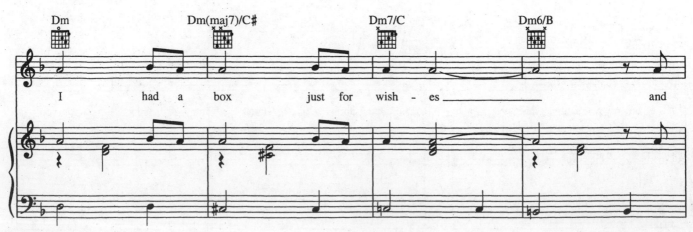

I had a box just for wish-es _____ and

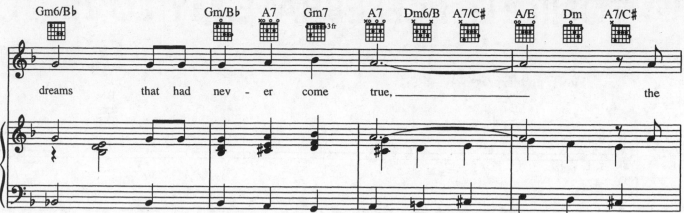

dreams that had nev-er come true, _____ the

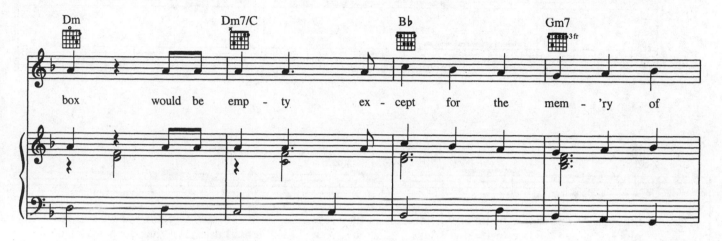

box would be emp-ty ex-cept for the mem-'ry of

how they were an-swered by you. _____ But there

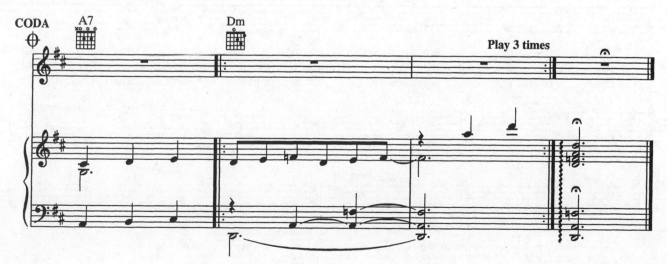

TONIGHT, I CELEBRATE MY LOVE

Music by MICHAEL MASSER
Lyric by GERRY GOFFIN

Slowly and Expressively

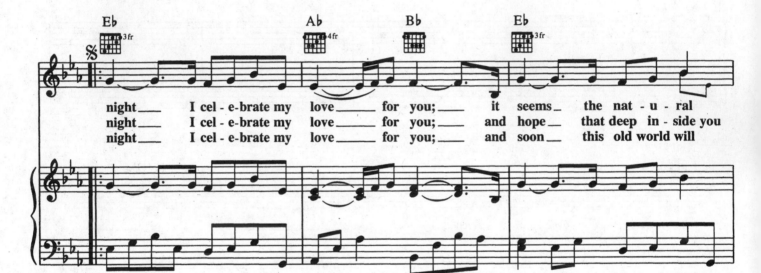

YOU ARE SO BEAUTIFUL

Words and Music by BILLY PRESTON
and BRUCE FISHER

VALENTINE

Words and Music by JACK KUGELL
and JIM BRICKMAN

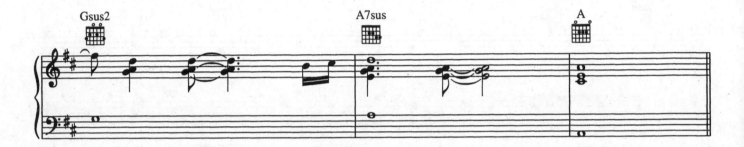

If there were no words, ___ no way to speak, ___ I ___
All of my life, ___ I have been wait - ing for ___ all ___

___ would still ___ hear ___ you. ___ If there were no tears, ___ no way to feel
___ you give ___ to ___ me. You've o - pened my eyes ___ and shown me how ___

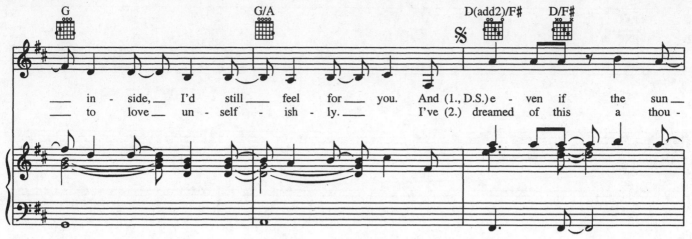

in - side,__ I'd still__ feel for__ you. And (1., D.S.) e - ven if ___ the sun __
to love__ un - self - ish - ly.___ I've (2.) dreamed of this ___ a thou -

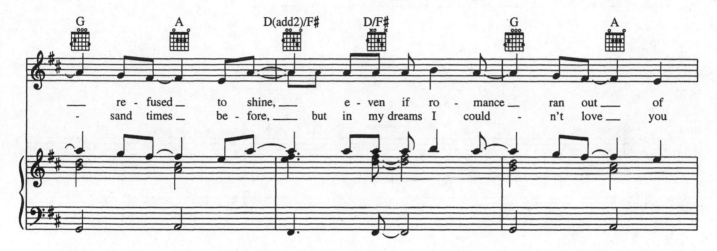

__ re - fused ___ to shine, ___ e - ven if ro - mance ___ ran out ___ of
- sand times ___ be - fore, ___ but in my dreams I could - n't love __ you

rhyme,   you would still have } my heart __ un - til ___ the end __ of time. __
more.   I will give you

(1., 2.) You're all I need, __ my love, ___ my val - en - tine.
(D.S.) 'Cause all I need ___ is you, __

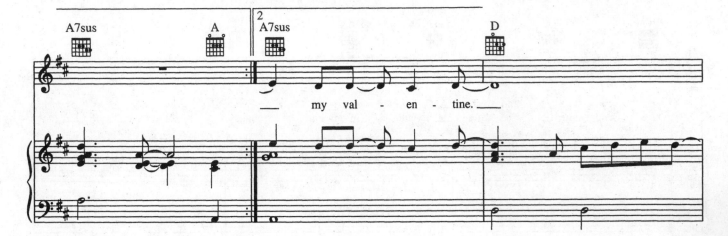

my val - en - tine.

La, la, la, la, la, la, la.

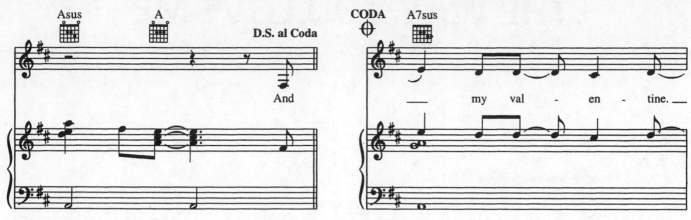

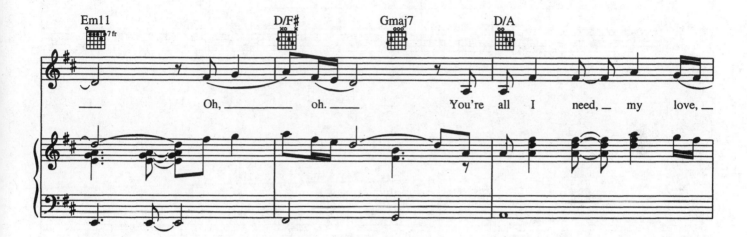

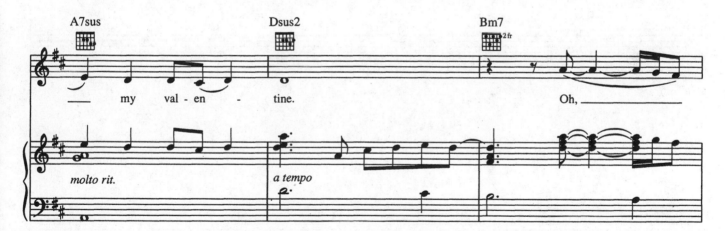

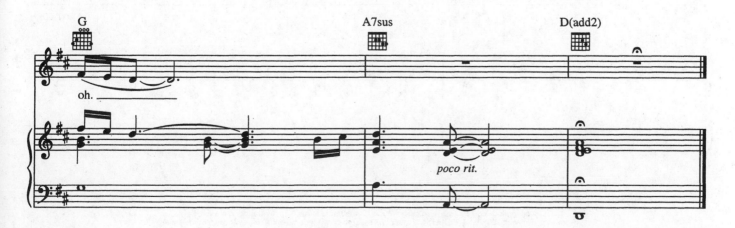

THE WAY YOU LOVE ME

Words and Music by MICHAEL DULANEY
and KEITH FOLLESE

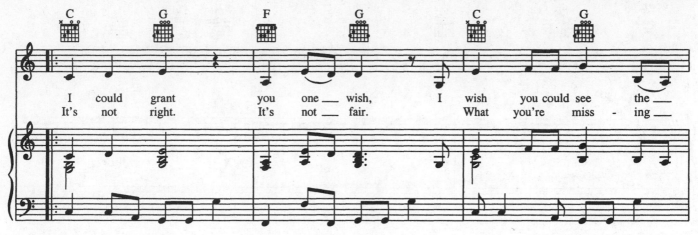

I could grant you one ___ wish, I wish you could see the ___
It's not right. It's not ___ fair. What you're miss - ing ___

way you ___ kiss. Ooh, ___ I love watch - ing you, ___ ba - by, ___
o - ver ___ there. Some - day I'll find a way to show ___ you ___

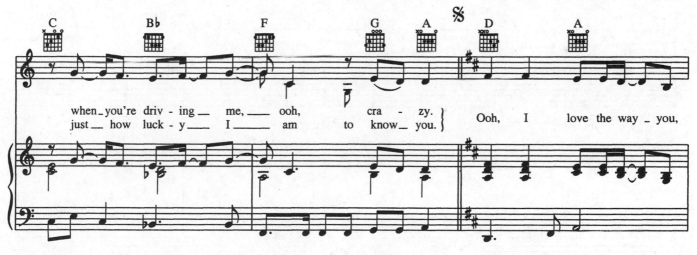

when ___ you're driv - ing ___ me, ___ ooh, cra - zy.
just ___ how luck - y ___ I ___ am to know ___ you. Ooh, I love the way ___ you,

love ___ the way ___ you love me. There's no - where else I'd rath - er be.
(When you touch me ___) (drives me wild. ___)

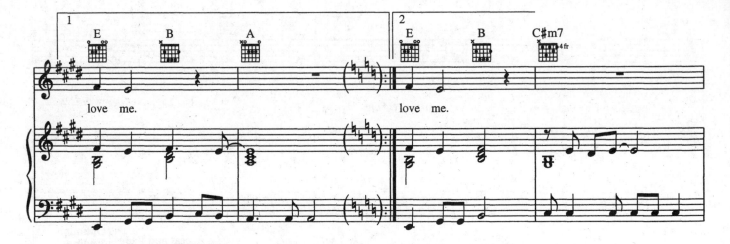

WEDDING BELL BLUES

Words and Music by
LAURA NYRO

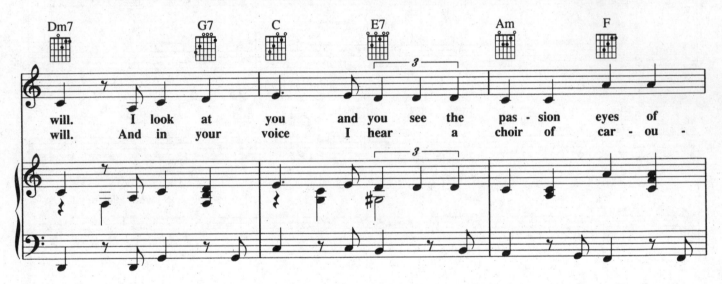

333

WONDERFUL TONIGHT

Words and Music by
ERIC CLAPTON

It's late in the eve - ning;
We go to a par - ty,
It's time to go home _ now,

she's won-d'ring what clothes _ to wear. _
and ev - 'ry - one turns _ to see _
and I've got an ach - ing head. _

She puts on her make -
this beau - ti - ful la -
So I give her the car _

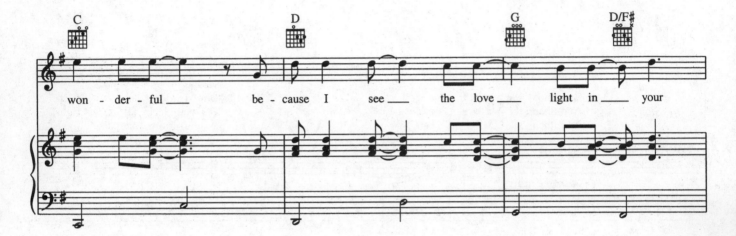

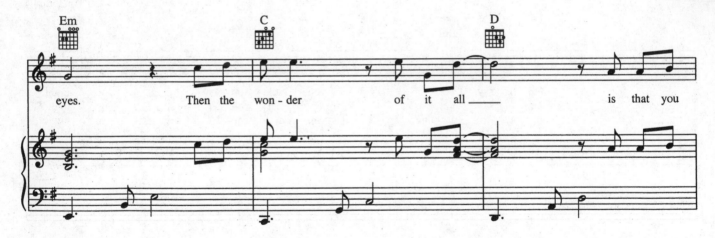

D.S. al Coda

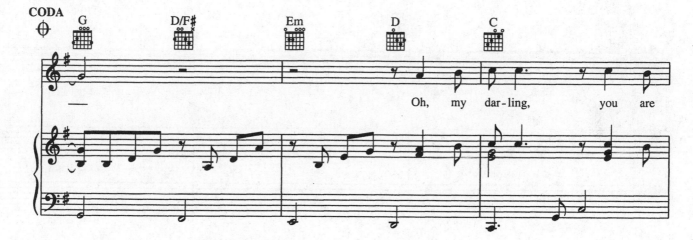

CODA

Oh, my dar-ling, you are

won - der - ful _____ to - night." __

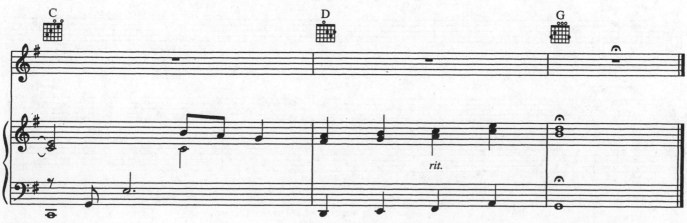

rit.

YOU ARE THE SUNSHINE OF MY LIFE

Words and Music by
STEVIE WONDER

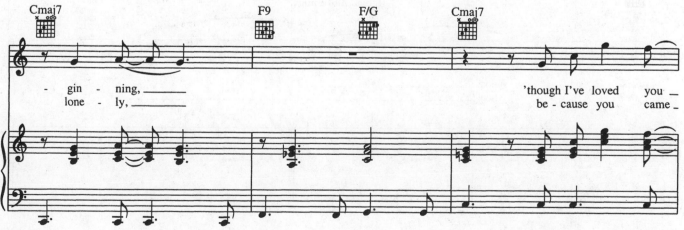

YOU DON'T HAVE TO BE A STAR
(To Be in My Show)

Words and Music by JOHN GLOVER
and JAMES DEAN

Relaxed Disco feel

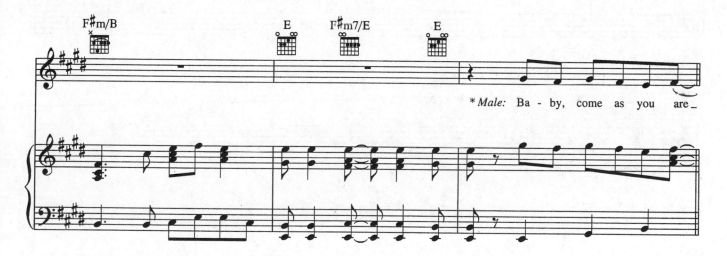

Male: Ba - by, come as you are _

— with just your heart, _ and I'll _ take you in. _

* *Male vocal written at pitch.*

You're re-ject-ed and hurt; _____ to me you're worth _

_ what you have with - in. _____

Female: Now I don't need _____ no su-per-star, _____ 'cause I'll ac-

cept you _____ as you are. ____ You won't be de-nied, ___ 'cause I'm sat-is-

fied __ with the love __ you __ in - spire. *Male:* You don't have to be a

star, ba - by, to be in my show. __

Female: You don't have to be a star, __ ba - by, to be in my __

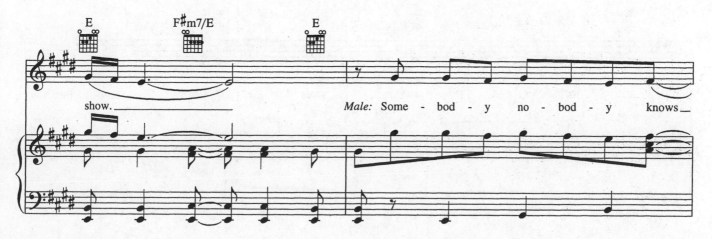

show. __ *Male:* Some - bod - y no - bod - y knows __

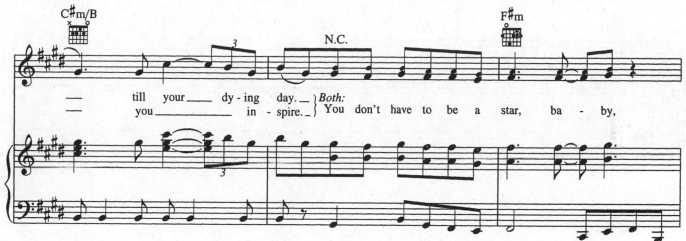

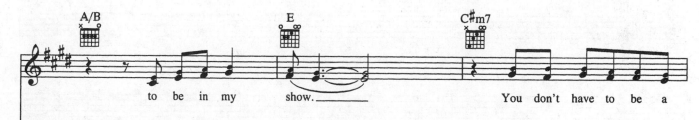

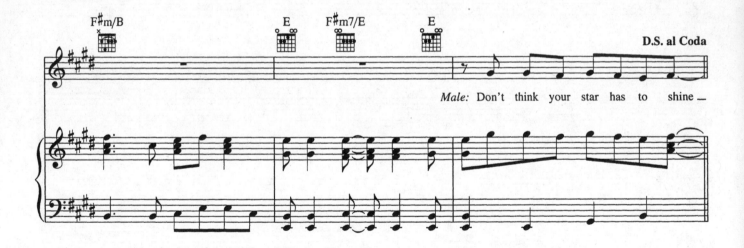

Male: Don't think your star has to shine ___

D.S. al Coda

CODA

to be in my   show. _____

YOU MEAN THE WORLD TO ME

Words and Music by BABYFACE,
L.A. REID and DARYL SIMMONS